NATURE AN[illegible] TRADITION

ARTS AND CRAFTS ARCHITECTURE [illegible] ND GUILDFORD

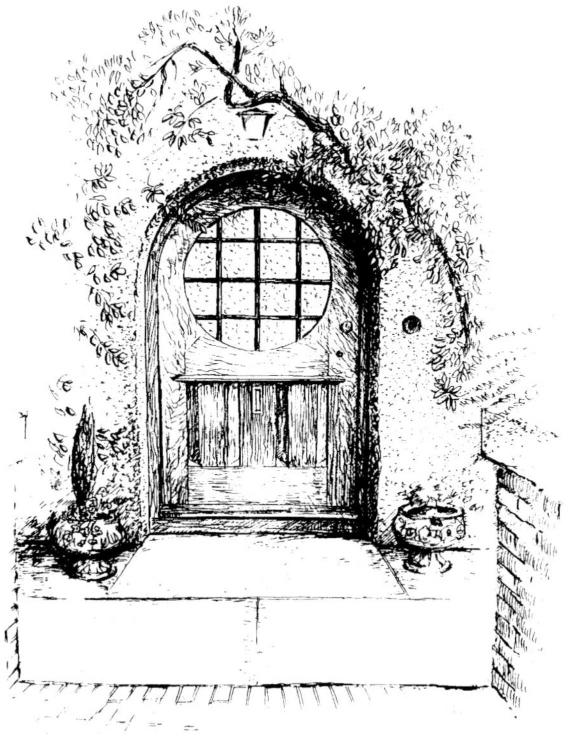

Sponsored by
The Arts and Crafts Movement
in Surrey
Guildford Borough Council

CONTENTS

INTRODUCTION TO THE SECOND EDITION

Since the original publication of *Nature and Tradition* in 1993, the Arts and Crafts Movement in Surrey has been formed as a society to promote appreciation, understanding and conservation of the buildings and gardens of the period. As Chairman of the Society, I am pleased to have the opporunity to introduce this second edition, which the Society is helping to fund.

The interest in all aspects of the Arts and Crafts Movement has grown considerably over the nine years since *Nature and Tradition* first appeared. The Guildford environs provide a marvellous showcase for a broad collection of buildings and gardens by most of the influential architects and garden designers of the period.

Of the original team who prepared the book, all except one continue to live and work in the area and have made an important contribution to increasing the awareness and understanding of the 'Arts and Crafts' period, through lectures, guiding tours and further research.

John George

ACKNOWLEDGEMENTS

The research team thanks all those who contributed material to help in the compilation of this book especially members and officers of Guildford Borough Council, Surrey County Council, the Guildford Society, Surrey Gardens Trust, the National Trust, the Lutyens Trust, the Society for the Protection of Ancient Buildings, staff of the Surrey Local Studies Library in Guildford and all owners of properties visited during the preparation of the book. If the research group has inadvertently failed to obtain any necessary permission, they offer sincere apologies. The views expressed are those of the authors of each section.

PHOTOGRAPHY AND ILLUSTRATIONS

The British Architectural Library, RIBA, London has permitted reproduction of drawings by Devey, Lutyens, Shaw and Voysey from its collection. Photographs are generally from collections at Guildford Borough Council, Surrey County Council, the British Library or by members of the research team. Original illustrations are by Boris Fijalkowski. Picture research by Sheila de Kretser. New illustrations on pages 53, 55 & 68 are by John Flower.

FOREWORD BY JANE BROWN

Author of "Gardens of a Golden Afternoon, the story of the partnership between Edwin Lutyens and Gertrude Jekyll' and a trustee of the Lutyens Trust.

There is perhaps nothing quite so fascinating as the domestic history of familiar ground; those of us who know and love present-day Guildford will applaud the appearance of this book. For newer residents and visitors it may well hold some intriguing surprises, for while Morris fabrics and wallpaper designs are widely appreciated as the legacy of the Arts and Crafts Movement, the houses and gardens are less well known. And yet, the arts of architecture and garden design flourished in England one hundred years ago just as gloriously as they did in the eighteenth century.

Just how many lovely houses and gardens came to be built in and around Guildford is explained in the following pages. Merilyn Spier, Nigel Barker, Brenda Lewis and Sheila de Kretser have researched and given generously of their expertise and familiarity with this area. They and their editor John Davey, symbolize some excellent teamwork, a positive collaboration between the guardians of both past and present, the Guildford Society, the Borough Council and Surrey County Council.

But another benevolent and ample presence is to be found hovering over these pages, that of the great gardener, Gertrude Jekyll. This year, 1993, is the 150th anniversary of Miss Jekyll's birth, and this book comes as a special tribute to her memory. She loved Guildford and belonged to this countryside, which she knew as 'Old West Surrey'. She was a consummate artist/craftswoman, believing fervently in the teachings of Ruskin and Morris (both of whom she knew) and she carried her beliefs into all the multifarious activities and friendships of her long life. She was brought up in Bramley and after youthful wanderings she settled at Munstead in the late 1870's. She became a familiar figure in Guildford and in the villages and lanes of the Wey Valley, driving her sprightly pony and blue cart, with her name painted on the back. Her artistic connections, her famous garden and her garden writing, and her busy nursery selling hardy plants and pot pourri, meant that she was known to everyone, from the venerable Watts at Compton to the prophet of a new art age, Roger Fry, who consulted her about his garden in Chantry View Road in 1910.

But Miss Jekyll had a particular appeal for young and clever architects, because she understood and appreciated their art and helped them with gardens for their houses. She introduced the young Edwin Lutyens to most of his clients in and around Guildford and her name is closely associated with his in their brilliant garden-making partnership. But she also encouraged and advocated the work of many others, notably C. F. A. Voysey, M. H. Baillie Scott and Thackeray Turner. Indeed, a conversation with Miss Jekyll lies behind the building of many of the houses mentioned in this book.

Gertrude Jekyll died in 1932, having bequeathed her "Old Surrey" collection to the Surrey Archaeological Society, now on permanent loan to the Museum at Castle Arch, where her famous gardening boots also reside. This book is an excellent introduction to her world of Guildford and its legacy from the Arts and Crafts Movement, and a fine anniversary tribute from one of the places she loved most.

Jane Brown.

1993

INTRODUCTION BY JOHN DAVEY

When I look back to the origins of this book, I'm sure that none of us who volunteered to contribute realized just how involved we would become with the subject.

The study is intended to provide a taste of the wealth of architecture and gardens which survive in the Guildford area from the period at the turn of the century when the Arts and Crafts Movement prospered. This area of Surrey is unique in having a broad collection of buildings from the period by the most influential architects.

The book was initially prompted when the Guildford Society contacted the Guildford Borough Council's Planning Division and suggested a publication on the Arts and Crafts buildings in Guildford Borough. Council officers had already looked at the Listed Buildings from this period in the Borough with the idea of publishing some form of guide. By linking up with the Guildford Society there was an opportunity to carry out a more detailed study. The Surrey County Council's Historic Buildings Advisor and Historic Gardens Officer also agreed to contribute and the scope of the study broadened to include gardens. As the name Gertrude Jekyll is synonymous with garden design of the period and 1993 is the 150th anniversary of her birth, there was an incentive to mark this event with a study of her work in the Guildford area adding to the content of the book. Although the book separates the architecture from the gardens, there is an obvious overlap and I hope the readers will appreciate this.

The study looks primarily at buildings and gardens within the Guildford Borough boundaries but, inevitably, properties close by could not be ignored and have been included where appropriate. Virtually all the examples in the text are listed buildings and therefore constitute the most important works of the period. It is hoped that by highlighting these properties, readers will develop an appreciation and ability to recognize the vast number of important Arts and Crafts buildings in the area.

I should like to thank all the patient owners of buildings and gardens who so enthusiastically assisted in our research and have allowed us to use photographs of their properties. It has not been possible to include all the research and findings in the book, but this is perhaps an excuse to produce volume II!

MEMBERS OF THE TEAM

Sheila de Kretser and Merilyn Spier – Guildford Society
Dr Nigel Barker and Brenda Lewis – Surrey County Council
John Davey, Editor – Guildford Borough Council

Summer-house by C. F. A. Voysey (1897) in the garden at Norney Grange.

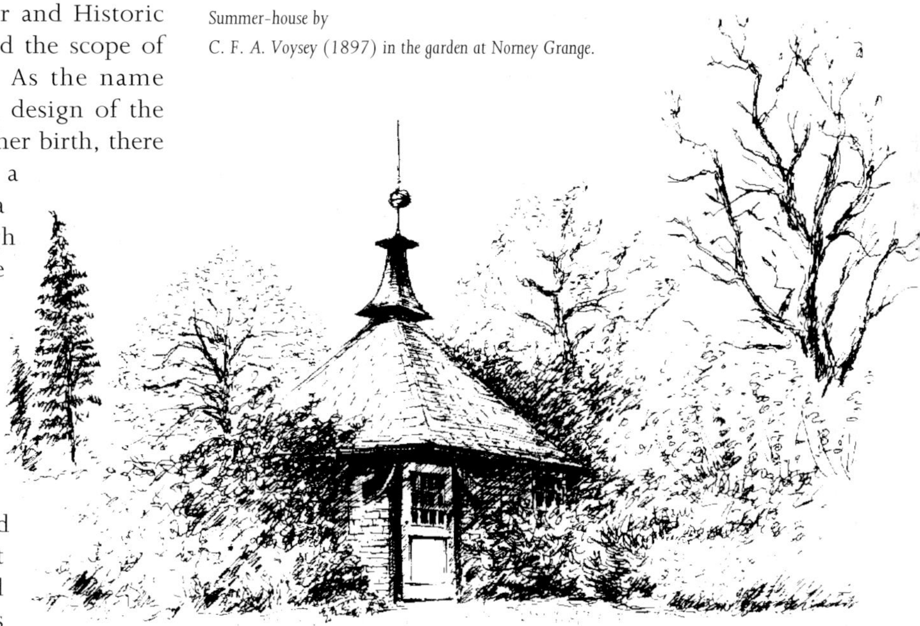

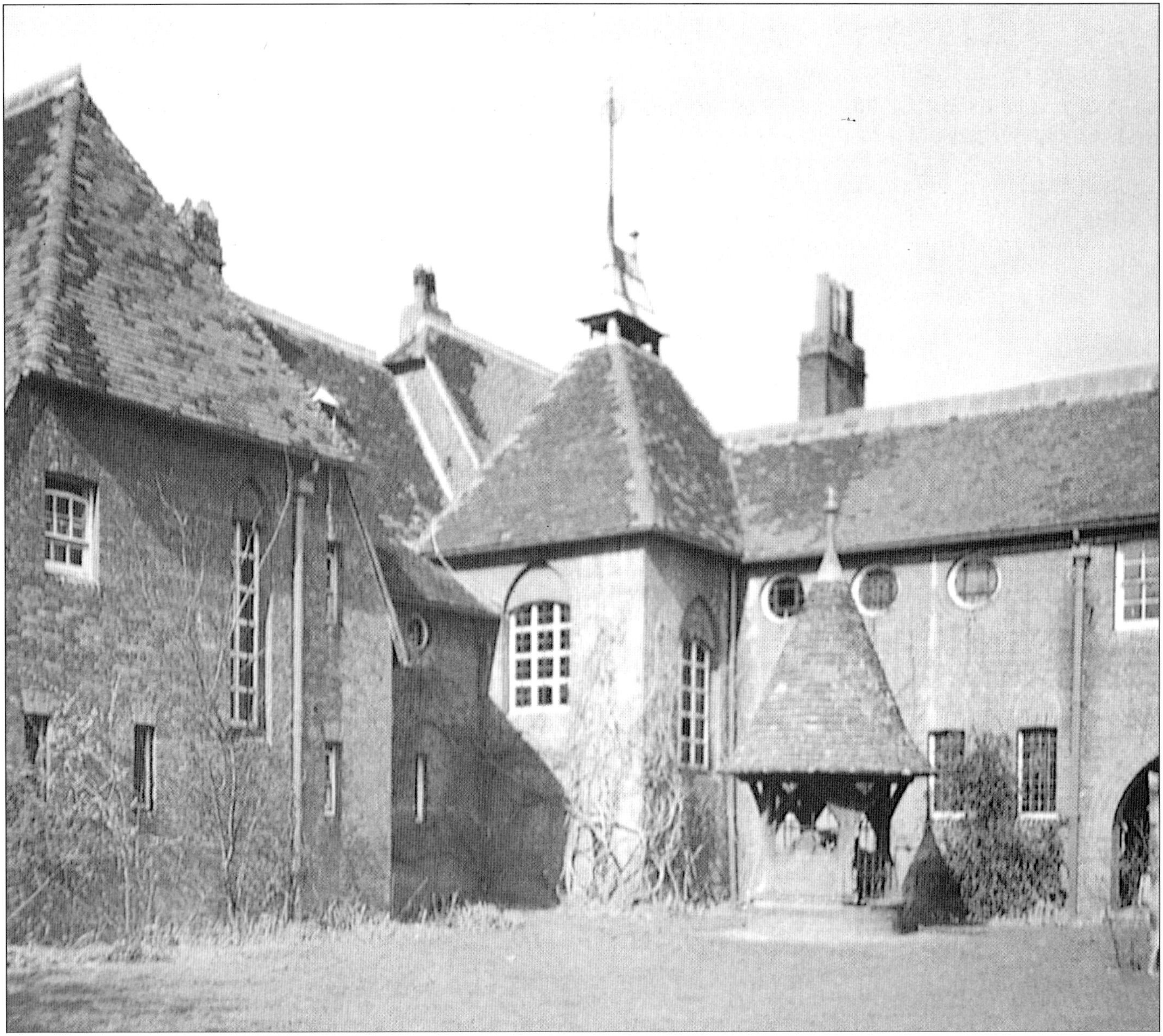

Fig. 1 *The Red House, Upton, Kent, (1859) by Philip Webb for William Morris.* (Courtesy of Elaine Harwood)

ARTS AND CRAFTS: THEORY AND PRACTICE

For about three decades at the turn of the century, the English Arts and Crafts Movement caught the attention of the western world. Its members were reacting against the stylistic excesses of the Victorian era and looked back to an idealized Medieval world in which the artist was also a craftsman, opposing the inhumanity of the Industrial Revolution. A whole generation of architects, artists and craftsmen was inspired by their ideals of truth to materials and function whilst creating freedom and originality in their designs.

> *"What I seek to show is that this Arts and Crafts movement is not what the Public has thought it to be, or is seeking to make it: a nursery for luxuries, a hothouse for the production of mere trivialities and useless things for the rich. To the men of this movement, who are seeking to compass the destruction of the commercial system, to discredit it, undermine it, overthrow it, their mission is just as serious and just as sacred as was that of their great grandfathers who first helped raise it into being, and thought that they had built for it an abiding monument in a crystal palace of glass and iron."*
>
> C. R. Ashbee: "Craftsmanship in Competitive Industry". 1908

In this address Ashbee, founder of the Guild of Handicrafts and the most original thinker of the Arts and Crafts Movement, summarized both the inspiration behind the movement that developed at the end of the nineteenth century and also the central paradox that it faced. In attempting to rediscover the unity between designer and craftsman and emphasizing this unity as the only method by which True Art would be created, the members of the movement limited their production, restricted their market and were subject to being caricatured as utopian dreamers hankering after an unobtainable bygone age. Although fervently believing that only by creating 'True Art' could the craftsman enrich society, the members of the Arts and Crafts Movement had an ambivalent attitude to mass manufacture that would allow their works, and therefore their ideals, to be disseminated to as wide an audience as possible; this originated from a fundamental opposition to what was seen as the dehumanizing industrialization that had evolved during the nineteenth century and a perception that the craftsman had become little more than a machine.

The origins of the Arts and Crafts Movement can be traced back to the writings of Augustus Welby Northmore Pugin (1812-52), an architect who championed the cause of Gothic architecture in his publications "Contrasts" and "The True Principles of Pointed or Christian Architecture". A convert to Catholicism, Pugin reacted against what he saw as the sacrilegious humanism of the eighteenth century, and its associated Classical architecture, advocating instead an idealized vision of Gothic architecture as the true national

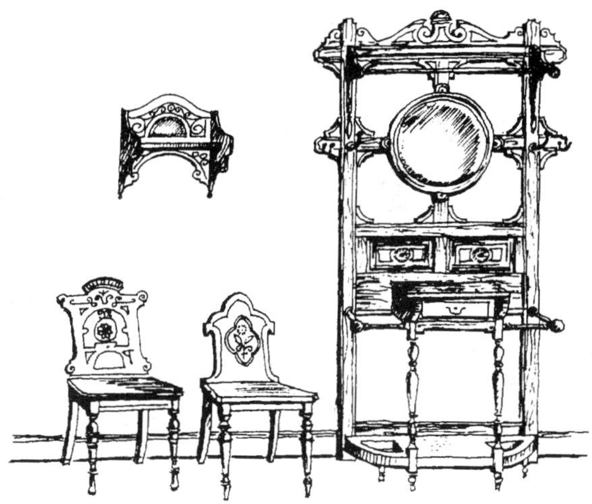

Fig. 2: An example of Victorian mass production against which the Arts and Crafts *Movement was reacting.*

style. He formed two great rules for design in "True Principles", which were:

> *"Have no features about a building which are not necessary for its convenience, construction or propriety; second, all ornament should consist of enrichment to the essential construction of the building.* (1)

Pugin was also involved in producing furniture and fittings for his buildings re-creating Gothic design and decoration to provide complete interiors. He exhibited examples in the Medieval Court at the Great Exhibition of 1851 at Crystal Palace.

For John Ruskin (1819-1900), the most influential of all Victorian writers on the arts, The Great Exhibition embodied the spiritual malaise that infected Britain in the nineteenth century. In its bewildering array of manufactured goods, produced without any concept of industrial design and with a variety of machined decorative finishes, the Crystal Palace appeared to be a temple to an industrial revolution that had severed workers from their formerly rural and agricultural existence and brought them into the sweatshops and slums of the industrial cities of England. In his most influential book "The Stones of Venice" of 1853, Ruskin produced an angry denunciation of the horrors of Victorian industrialization that was to be the basis of the Arts and Crafts Movement:

> *"...you must either make a tool of the creature, or a man of him – you cannot make both. Men were not intended to work with the accuracy of tools, to be precise and perfect in all their actions – if you will have all that precision out of them, and make their fingers measure degrees like cog-wheels, and their arms strike curves like compasses you must unhumanize them."*

Ruskin believed man-made articles should reveal rather than disguise their origins and that individuality and roughness of workmanship was better than perfection and standardization. He saw art and manufacture and its lack of direction and cohesion as a public concern and taught that it was not enough to turn your back on mechanization. The defects in society that had produced such goods had to be tackled. Ruskin believed that every man should work for his living, preferably for some of the time with his hands; thus elevating the craft aesthetic to a central role in society and arguing that the example of the Medieval artisan was the one to follow. Ruskin was equally clear in his support of the Pre-Raphaelite Brotherhood of Painters, contrasting their brightness of colour and directness of observation with the darker, more academic and established Old Master tradition of the Royal Academy, and particularly commending the Pre-Raphaelites' study of nature. It was Ruskin's writings, particularly his essay on "The Nature of Gothic" contained within "The Stones of Venice" that were to have the most profound influence on the central, inspirational figure of the Arts and Crafts Movement – William Morris.

WILLIAM MORRIS

Morris was of genteel bourgeois stock, the son of a widow with a private income. A sickly child who immersed himself in romantic Medievalizing novels, he grew into a sturdy energetic man with a private income of some £900 a year that allowed him freedom to choose his vocation, initially that of the Church. It was whilst at Oxford, where he met Edward Burne-Jones, that he first encountered the writings of Ruskin and fired by enthusiasm he changed vocation to architecture, entering the office of the great High Victorian architect George Edmund Street. Famous as a Gothic Revivalist producing sumptuous multicoloured interiors, Street was also interested in furnishings, fittings, paintings, fabrics and stained glass, a significant fact when considering Morris's later career. Although known for his hard muscular Gothic style, Street had an abiding concern for honest use of materials and careful craftsmanship that was to influence his many pupils, who included Philip Webb (1831-1915) and Richard Norman Shaw (1831-1912).

Morris was only in Street's Office for approximately nine months, where he was mainly engaged on drawing studies of buildings and their details before deciding that he wanted to be a painter, which he was to find equally difficult. He was inspired in this choice by meeting Dante Gabriel Rossetti – a member of the Pre-Raphaelite Brotherhood, whose later relationship with Jane Burden (Mrs Morris) was to complicate Morris's life and cause him much pain. It was however, during this period that Morris met and became friends with many of the up and coming generation of artists and architects, one of his most important friendships being that with Philip Webb, chief clerk to Street.

It was Webb who designed the Red House, Upton, Kent, for Morris; a project they discussed at length whilst travelling together in a boat on the Seine, and a building which shows the influence of Street on both the younger men. Although elevated by later followers as a great Arts and Crafts house, it was not an innovative design in itself, being a continuation of the Gothic Revival evident in the contemporary vicarages of both Street and Butterfield, and Morris himself called it "a house in the style of the thirteenth century". Where it is significant is in the fact that it was built as a country house for a gentleman of means, which was to be the characteristic type of patron for later Arts and Crafts architects. Also Morris insisted that the Red House, sited in an orchard, should be placed so that very few trees would have to be felled. Thus house and garden were part of the alliance of art and nature that was to become a central part of Arts and Crafts belief. Internally Morris visualized the house as a re-interpretation of the received ideas of High Victorian design, although the furniture and fittings provided by Webb were simple. It was clearly a major factor in Morris realizing his talent for design and the decorative arts that led him to establish in 1860 Morris, Marshall, Faulkner and Co – fine art workmen specializing in painting, carving furniture and the metals; "a manufactory of all things necessary for the decoration of a house".

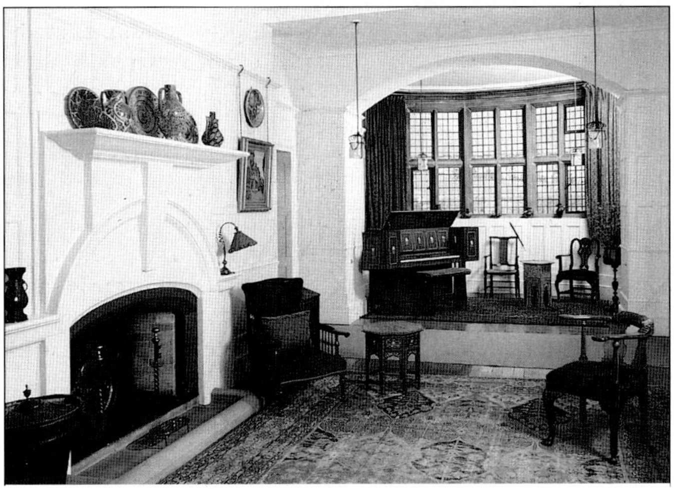

Fig. 3: The Hall at Standen by Philip Webb,(1892). Courtesy of the National Trust

The success of the company in exhibiting its products in the 1862 International Exhibition, was such that Morris had to reconcile the business requirements of efficient and cost effective supply with his belief in the integrity of the craftsman. It was only with the establishment of Morris and Co in Oxford Street in 1876, as successor to Morris, Marshall, Faulkner and Co, that he achieved this. Morris was not implacably opposed to the machine, he objected to it being exploited for profit over quality, thus degrading the work of the craftsman. Although he stressed a co-operative organic approach, in reality, Morris created both at his Merton Abbey works and Kelmscott Manor, communities of craftsmen/labourers who worked under his supervision to realize his most famous rule, expounded in his lecture "The Beauty of Life" which was:

> *"Have nothing in your houses that you do not know to be useful or believe to be beautiful."*

It was with the creation of the guild movement in the 1880's that the term Arts and Crafts became used. Although Ruskin had founded his idea of a Medieval guild in the mid-nineteenth century – The Guild of St George – it was not until 1883 that a group of architectural students and assistants in the Office of Richard Norman Shaw formed the

Guild of Handicraftsmen and Designers in the Arts. The Century Guild was formed to make all branches of Art the responsibility of the Artist and also called for the marriage of Art and Industry. The Art Workers Guild, formed in 1884, emerged from a combination of young architects led by W.R. Lethaby, who felt separated from craftsmen by the business of trade. This led in turn in 1888 to the formation of the Arts and Crafts Exhibition Society, to provide a forum for the promotion and display to the public of what the writer Cobden Sanderson dubbed Arts and Crafts Movement design. It can be fairly said that members of the guild movement were the inheritors to Morris, young men who were becoming interested in the interrelationship between material, working process and aesthetic form. Debate within the Guilds concentrated on the importance of Arts to modern life with the moral aim of stripping out purely decorative elements from design and reusing traditional motifs in a simplified manner. Morris himself was slightly reserved about the Arts and Crafts Movement as he did not want to divorce the revival of skills from his equal desire to reform society.

ARTS AND CRAFTS ARCHITECTURE

The role of architecture within the guilds, which were primarily concerned with the decorative arts, was problematic. However, the importance of architecture as the setting for all the other arts, was acknowledged by all members of the movement, many of whom were trained as architects. The problem with architectural training and practice was that it had to be done at a distance, based largely on drawing existing buildings. The concern of the Arts and Crafts Movement was the drift in architectural training into separate academic disciplines of Architecture, Sculpture and Painting, and their desire was to reunite all aspects of design into the one, based primarily on a study of vernacular traditions. As T.G. Jackson observed in 1890,

"For though the advantages of pupilage or apprenticeship are so great that they are not likely to be given up, still the student must of necessity supplement the experience gained in his master's office by study and reading of his own, and the office is and should be to him rather the place where he may expect to see put into practice the lessons he has learnt elsewhere, rather than the place where he can expect to be taught directly everything he ought to know. He has, therefore to join classes at Art School and to enter on a course of reading, sketching and independent study of his own"

For Philip Webb, W. Lethaby, Voysey and Lutyens it was the less academic and more practical approach that was the most important. The study of local building traditions and their use of local materials were of paramount importance. Lutyens for example spent his youth studying the picturesque cottages of south-west Surrey, tracing them onto a small piece of framed glass with slices of soap he had cut to a sharp edge. He also spent considerable time at the village carpenter's shop in Thursley and Tickner's builders yard in Godalming learning the practical aspects of building construction. Similarly, Philip Webb considered that true architecture was in the art of common, or traditional building and the honest use of local materials. It was this approach that led to the distinctive design of the Arts and Crafts house.

THE ARTS AND CRAFTS HOUSE

Siting was particularly important in the Arts and Crafts house and a gentle undulating landscape was preferred. The house was usually sited on an unspoilt, frequently wooded, south facing slope so that it could hug the contours and ideally appear as if it had grown organically from the land. Frequently the house was of medium size, more a house in the country than a true country house with extensive services. It was intended as the idyllic country retreat for the wealthy upper middle classes within easy reach of the main city centre, and it is surely significant that the majority of them are located in the Home Counties around London. The relationship between house and garden was particularly important, with the use of terraces and planting to integrate the building into the landscape.

The idea of linking house and garden was one explored by some of the garden authors of the time including Thomas Mawson, who wrote "The Art and Craft of Garden Making" in 1900. He believed that the English vernacular was rooted in an awareness of the landscape and that buildings should be integrated within the wider context of planting, an alternative tradition being that of the old-fashioned garden that was enclosed and independent from the broader landscape. A house could not be designed without due regard for site, materials, climate, some knowledge of garden craft and the natural habitat of trees and plants if both house and garden were to be seen to belong to the soil – the ultimate aim of both the Arts and Crafts architect and the garden designer.

If there is such a thing as a typical Arts and Crafts house, which is difficult to claim as they were meant to reflect local building traditions and would therefore vary from area to area, its main characteristic would be a deceptively simple exterior. However, it would be full of subtle details which were the result of either practical construction or based on observation of traditional practice. Thus at The Lodge in Shere, designed by Lutyens for the Bray Estate in 1894, the local sandstone is used for the ground floor, and the first floor jetties or projects forward. There is a large stack typical of many old Surrey houses, although here Lutyens has, with his typical inventiveness, made the stack the centre of the composition. *(See Fig. I Colour illustration of The Lodge at Shere)*

Small refinements such as exposed rafter feet or simple porch hoods are often missed in a cursory glance with many houses of this type as they have been seen before and in themselves they may not be remarkable. However, it is because they are traditional features that they are comforting and taken for granted. The interiors were similarly deceptively simple. The horizontal emphasis of many of the houses produced a feeling of intimacy, but any sense of oppression was relieved by the more extensive use of windows, usually leaded casements, and often with deep reveals. The fixtures of windows and doors were usually where the decorative imagination was allowed to play, the other important area being the fireplace. The use of a large and often elaborate fireplace, either in brick and stone, or with cast iron and decorative tiles, emphasized the intended comfort of the Arts and Crafts house and the idea of hearth and home, with every fixture having the appearance of being handcrafted and especially designed for the house.

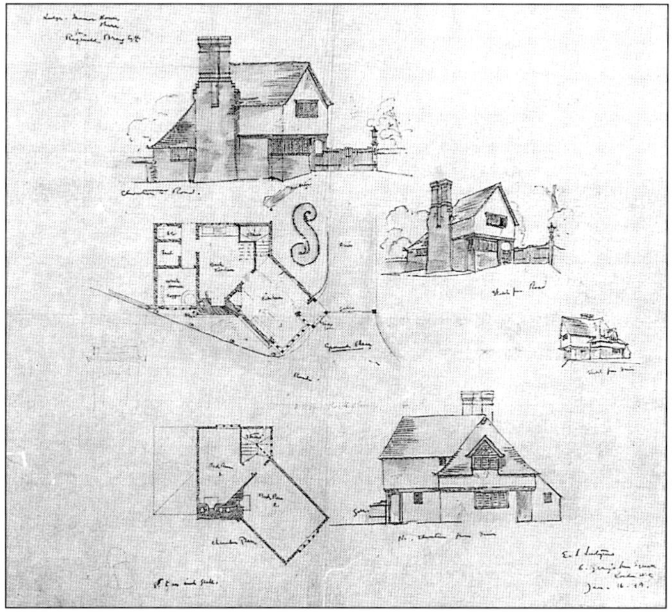

Fig. 4: Sketches by Lutyens for The Lodge at Shere of 1894
Courtesy of the British Architectural Library RIBA

The development of the house in the country as an informal, idyllic retreat from the city, in no recognizable formal style reached its height in the last years of the nineteenth century and in the period around 1900. Surrey was visited by many foreign architects interested in the new developments in domestic buildings. Perhaps one of the most well known of these visitors was Hermann Muthesius, an architect and attaché to the German embassy in London, who left a graphic account of his impressions:

> *"Exemplary qualities in the English House: English Houses, as we can see, are wisely reduced to essentials and adapted to given circumstances; the point, therefore, that is worth copying from them is the emphasis that is laid on purely objective requirements. The Englishman builds his house for himself alone. He feels no urge to impress, has no thought of festive occasions or banquets and no idea of shining in the eyes of the world through lavishness in and of his house simply does not occur to him. Indeed, he even avoids attracting attention to his house by means of striking design or architectonic extravagance, just as he would be loath to appear personally eccentric by wearing a fantastic suit. It is most instructive to note at this point that a movement opposing the imitation of styles and seeking closer ties with simple rural buildings, which began over forty years ago, has had the most gratifying results. This same down to earth quality which we see in the design of the house is apparent too in its siting and the way in which it relates to the country around it. The aim is to adapt the house closely to its surroundings and attempt to make house and garden into a unified, closely-knit whole. A fairly recent movement in garden design has revolutionized the surroundings of the house and in particular has removed from the scene the erroneous views of impersonal landscape gardening. Like the changes to the exterior, changes to the interior of the house have simplicity, objectivity, plainness (sic) and unobtrusive comfort as their aim."* (2)

It was the obvious interest in honest, local building traditions and the English love of the countryside expressed in the Arts and Crafts house and garden that so struck foreign visitors. It is perhaps significant that in the current reaction against "High Tech" living and style that has become evident in recent years there is a parallel to the views of earlier generations in the nineteenth century and the appeal of the Arts and Crafts is becoming increasingly popular; representing as it does the unity between nature and tradition that appears to be an integral part of the British character.

NOTES TO TEXT:

(1) "True Principles of Christian or Pointed Architecture" by A.W.N. Pugin, published in 1841. Pugin's father, Augustus Charles, was a draughtsman in the Office of John Nash and was later editor of a number of books on Gothic architecture, on which Pugin the younger assisted. A.W.N. Pugin designed furniture for Windsor Castle and stage sets for the theatre before he was twenty. A convert to Catholicism in 1834, he had a turbulent private life including being shipwrecked, married three times and eventually losing his mind in 1851. He leapt to fame and notoriety in 1836 with the publication of "Contrasts" – a plea for Catholicism and illustrated by comparisons between mean eighteenth century or contemporary buildings contrasted with the richness and glories of Gothic architecture from the Catholic past. "True Principles" was a greater exploration of the connections between the Gothic style and structure and the function of each component, hence its influence on later architectural thinking.

(2) "Das Englische Haus' by Hermann Muthesius originally published by Wasmuth, Berlin in 1904, 1905 (three volumes) Reprinted and translated 1979 Crosby Lockwood Staples. Granada Publishing Ltd. Part I: Development. Introduction pp 10-11.

ARTS AND CRAFTS ARCHITECTURE IN AND AROUND GUILDFORD

For a brief period in the 1890's England, and in particular the South-East, was leading the world in developing a new aesthetic movement which was free from stylistic references and fostered buildings which were practical, comfortable and uplifting to the human spirit. The movement's architects used traditional building techniques with handcrafted details and local building materials wherever possible. The internal arrangement of the building was allowed to determine its external form to a greater extent which often resulted in an asymmetrical, picturesque appearance, as found historically in the vernacular buildings of the countryside. It was often the humbler type of house that was the model drawn upon by leading architects of the movement including Sir Edwin Lutyens, Charles Voysey, Thackeray Turner and Baillie Scott. Surrey and the area around Guildford is rich with work of these architects as well as those of the earlier generation who influenced the Arts and Crafts Movement, including George Devey, Philip Webb, Sir Ernest George and Richard Norman Shaw.

THE TRANSFORMATION OF A COUNTRY TOWN

By the time the London & South-Western Railway arrived in Guildford in May 1845, the town had a population of about 5,000. Fifty years later in 1895, the population had grown to approximately 15,000 residents, the majority of whom were recent immigrants to the area. Before the advent of the railway, Guildford was a relatively self-sufficient market town situated midway between London and the south coast. The town's main source of extra revenue was catering to the travellers who found it convenient to break their journeys at one of its six coaching inns. The railway brought about the demise of that trade but introduced to the town the low paid construction workers, followed by the professional classes who found that they could live a country lifestyle whilst working in the capital. Now on the main line and in an easily accessible, unspoilt area, Guildford was an attractive choice for those wishing to build on its southern margins, where there were fine views over the valleys beyond. An aerial view of Surrey today would show a string of comfortable and substantial late nineteenth century houses, occupying the hills above the southern facing slopes stretching from Caterham in the east to Haslemere in the south-west. Builders and landowners alike recognized the commercial opportunities of the area as is demonstrated in a Directory of 1870 which stated that:

> "*City men might find in the suburbs of Guildford elegant residences within easy distance of their place of business...*" (1)

The compact market town and its surrounding villages where traditional practical skills for living and working still survived, was subject to an influx of urbane newcomers, a totally different breed from the peasants and landowners traditional to the area. The newcomers looked out from the town towards the city for their employment, rather than looking into Guildford itself. They were largely upper middle class professionals and successful artists, people who could be receptive to exploring contemporary ideas in domestic design to reflect their lifestyles. Some were attracted to the idealistic principles behind the Arts and Crafts Movement whilst others may have found that the informal and picturesque appearance of many Arts and Crafts buildings simply looked right in a country setting.

The buildings, their architects and clients will generally be presented in chronological order to enable the reader to build up a picture of the changes of ideas and tastes during the period from 1875 to 1910.

THE FORERUNNERS TO THE ARTS AND CRAFTS MOVEMENT IN GUILDFORD

RICHARD NORMAN SHAW (1831-1912)

Richard Norman Shaw was one of the first Victorian architects to study traditional English rural architecture and re-interpret it for contemporary use, creating what has become known as "The Old English Style", considered to be a precursor to the Arts and Crafts Movement. He was a highly successful and talented London architect whose office was the breeding ground for many of the Arts and Crafts architects of the following generation. After his own training in the offices of three of the most prestigious High Victorian architects – William Burn, Anthony Salvin and George Edmund Street, Shaw and his partner-to-be, William Eden Nesfield, went on an intensive sketching trip to Kent where they studied vernacular cottages and their building techniques. In 1862, Shaw set up in practice and embarked on a very successful career, building country houses in the "Old English Style", town houses in the "Queen Anne Style", churches in a "Neo-Gothic" style and his final public buildings at the turn of the century in a flamboyant, "Neo-Baroque" style. (2) Shaw is said to have had his shirts made with extra long cuffs to enable him to draw a prospective building on them for a potential client whilst at the dining table, an anecdote which demonstrates his versatility, business acumen and social skills.

Shaw's practice attracted clients who wished to build substantial houses within easy travelling distance of the capital and, fortunately, Guildford has several examples. His earliest work in the Guildford area, at Worplesdon, is Merrist Wood House of 1877, situated on a fine site looking south towards the Hog's Back. This moderately sized house is one of his first to combine tile-hanging, half-timbering and Bargate stone, (a local material), in an informal composition which became the hallmark of his 'Old English Style'. The entrance elevation has a prominent porch and large chimney stack. A pretty pair of half-timbered lodges with dominant central chimney-stacks flank the entrance drive. Now part of Merrist Wood Agricultural College, much interior alteration has taken place in the main house which was partially rebuilt following a fire in 1978.

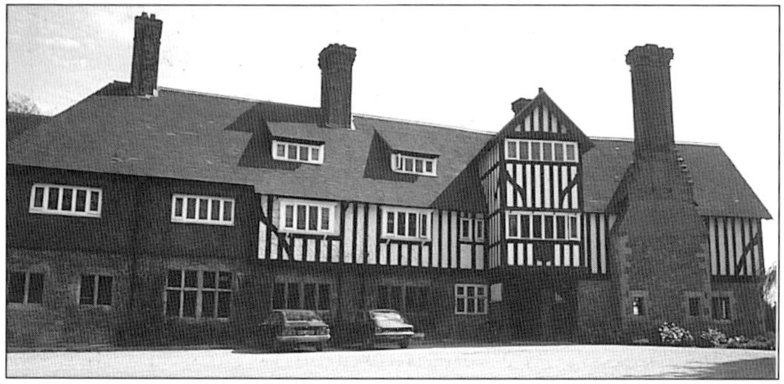

Fig. 5: Front elevation of Merrist Wood House (1877) by Richard Norman Shaw.

A year later Norman Shaw employed the same builder, Frank Birch of Farnham, to build Piccards Rough in St Catherine's, an imposing mansion commissioned by Thomas Wilde Powell, one time mayor of Guildford. Built mainly of Bargate stone and plain roughcast walls under slate roofs, the house has a baronial appearance. The materials are a departure from the 'Old English' half-timber and tile, but other trademarks of the Shaw style are present. The house is an asymmetrical composition under a complex roofline with many gables outlined by bold bargeboards and massive brick stacks. The leaded casement windows are of traditional design and are picturesquely random. Internally, the space is well organized with a clear hierarchy of family rooms grouped together, separate from the servants quarters and stables. The stable block still contains its patterned block floors and original stalls. The house also has an early use of concealed steel beams which Shaw used to provide smaller rooms on the first floor over the larger family spaces below.

Lodges, built as part of the estate are examples of traditional cottages re-interpreted by Shaw. The importance of the garden in the planning of country houses cannot be over-estimated, and here at Piccards Rough a stone terrace cut into the hillside affords views over the southern slopes, enhanced by formal planting to allow private views from within, through the leaded casements of the family rooms. The house was divided in the 1950's when a section was demolished and the garden was subdivided.

There are a number of smaller houses by Shaw along the Portsmouth Road in Guildford. Dating from 1883, no's. 87-91 are a pair of large semi-detached houses which again illustrate Shaw's 'Old English Style' with brick and tile hung elevations, wide bargeboards to the gables, imposing brick chimneys and steeply pitched clay tile roofs. Hitherbury House, further south along the Portsmouth Road is of similar character, but has been greatly altered over recent years. In the shallow dip of the Portsmouth Road at St Catherine's as it leaves Guildford, and hidden behind an archway, stands a picturesque group of eight 'Old English Style' cottages in two blocks of four. The arched building fronting the road was originally a Working Man's Club, now converted into a house. This small 'estate', named The Valley, dates from 1881 and is a delightful combination of half-timbering and tile-hanging over brick, very much in the style of Norman Shaw, but probably by one of his gifted pupils rather than the master himself. *(See Fig III Colour illustration of The Valley)*

Outside Guildford itself, in the attractive countryside near Shere, is Burrows Cross of 1885. This house and lodge with its tile-hung and brick elevations were built as a country retreat for Frank Holl, a successful artist. After Holl's death in 1889, the new owner, artist Benjamin Leader, commissioned Shaw to design additions to both sides of the entrance to form further studio space. Both the house and lodge had several details which also appear in Lutyen's Surrey work, for example the use of protruding tiles to deflect water from window heads, windows wrapping themselves around corners and the informal arrangement of two and three storey sections under picturesque rooflines. Like Piccards Rough, Burrows Cross has now been subdivided into three units.

Towards the end of the century, works by other leading architects of the period were also appearing in and around Guildford and its pleasant countryside, many showing evidence of study of the vernacular architecture of old England. Guildford does not on the whole have examples of the enormous and opulent mansions built for Victorian Magnates, nor does it tell the whole story of the Arts and Crafts, but it does have a wide range of examples of the

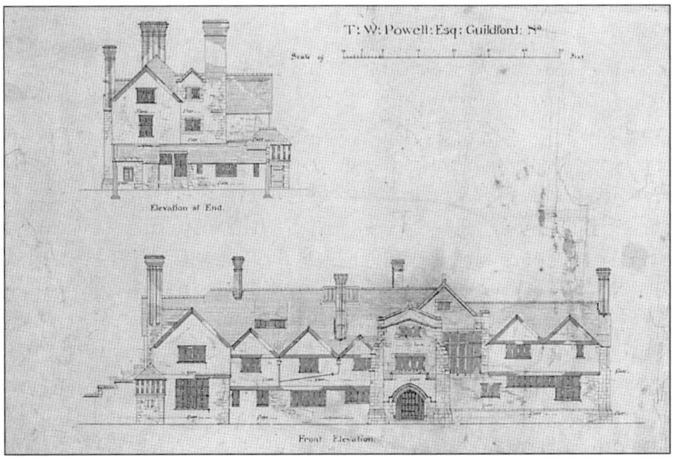

Fig. 6: Drawing from Norman Shaw's office of Piccards Rough (1878) Showing front and side elevations (Courtesy of the British Architectural Library RIBA)

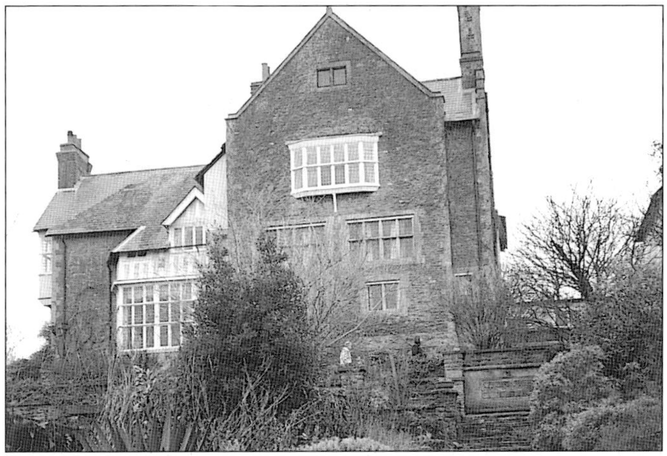

Fig. 7: Garden elevation of Piccards Rough as it is today

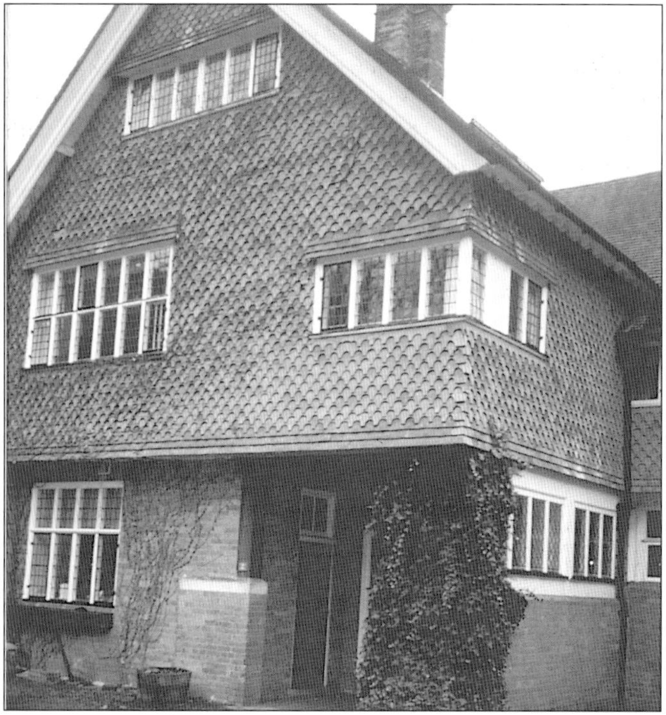

Fig. 8: *View of Burrows Cross (1885) by Richard Norman Shaw*

'house in the country' that was used for entertaining and suited to the professional and artistic classes.

GEORGE DEVEY (1820-1886)

A highly successful 'country house' architect who started in practice in the 1840's, Devey concentrated exclusively on building country houses with a Jacobean or Tudor flavour for a clientele of bankers and the aristocracy. Throughout his career he avoided publicity, never allowing his designs to be published. A watercolourist by early training, he produced several volumes of sketches of details of traditional sixteenth and seventeenth century English buildings. Devey attempted to translate this local vernacular, the result of gradual accretions and extensions over time, into more substantial houses on a grand scale designed to meet the modern needs of his wealthy clients. In 1871, Devey designed Send Holme near Guildford for Captain W. Hargreaves. This imposing brick and stone mansion was built in the Jacobean manner,with stepped gables and massive chimneys. Walls begin in the local Bargate stone, but then gradually change to brick, with diapering (or criss-cross patterning) modelled on the sixteenth and seventeenth century country house. Windows of varying sizes have Bargate stone surrounds. This artificially picturesque approach to materials was repeated by Devey throughout his career. *(See Fig II Colour illustration Watercolour of Send Holme).*

Internally, the main living rooms are arranged informally and are very large, lit by great bay windows, and are decorated with Jacobean style oak wall panelling and wooden strapwork ceilings. It is extremely fortunate that Send Holme stands largely unchanged today with much of its interior intact, unlike another Devey house, Monkshatch. Built in 1885 on the slopes of the Hog's Back above Compton, Monkshatch was designed for the President of the Stock Exchange, Andrew Hitchens, whose wife was a great friend of the artist G.F. Watts. All that remains of the estate today are the garden walls and a small garden pavilion in a serious state of disrepair.

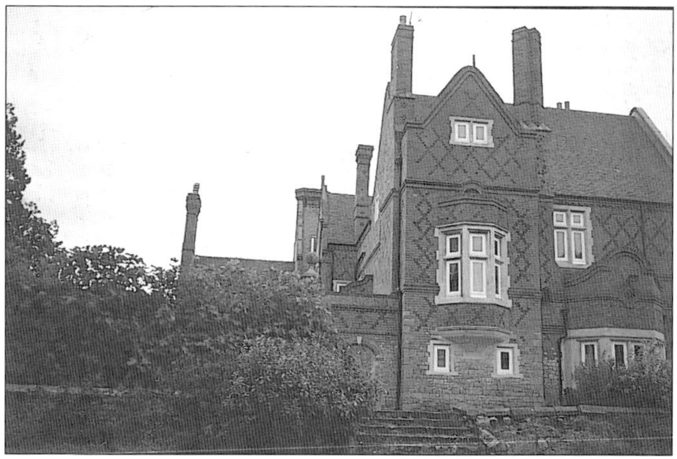

Fig. 9: *The side elevation of Send Holme by George Devey,(1871).*

SIR ERNEST GEORGE (1839-1922)

A London based architect who had varied commissions for churches, houses, public and commercial buildings in the capital, he also worked in several country towns and the countryside of the South-East. He and his partners designed in a variety of styles to suit location and customer, but favoured the "Queen Anne" style. Examples of his work in Guildford include The Hillier Almshouses of 1879 on the Farnham Road and now largely demolished apart from a summer house and pavilion. He also designed Cranley Cottages and Lodge (1884), a picturesque pair of semi-detached, half-timbered cottages in the 'Old English' style at West Clandon.

A later work was Limnerslease of 1891 which is a large rambling country house in Compton with 'fake' half-timbered elevations. The timber is fixed to brickwork with roughcast 'infill'. This deceit was necessary because of newly enacted bye-laws that forbade traditional half-timber construction with flammable infill. The house was designed for the artist G.F. Watts and his devoted wife Mary, whose presence in Compton is a separate story unique to Guildford.
(See p34 and Fig X Colour illustration of Limnerslease, Compton)

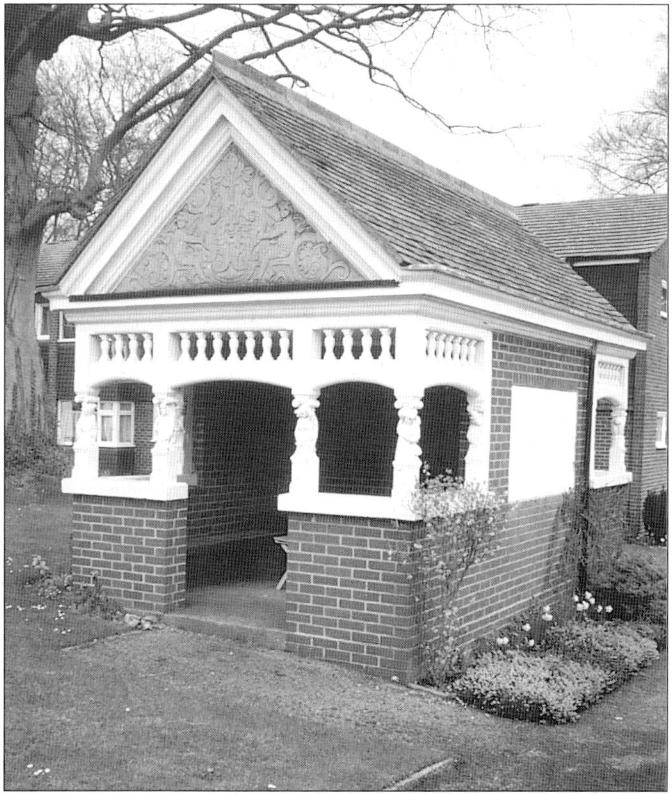

Fig. 10 Summer House (1879), originally part of Hillier's Almshouses by Sir Ernest George.

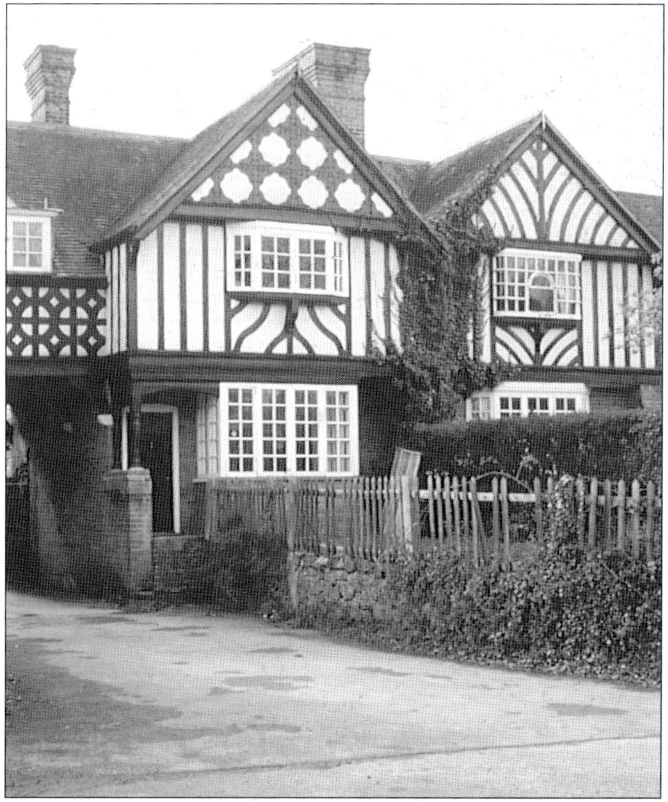

Fig. 11 Cranley Cottages (1884) a pair of 'Old English' semi-detached cottages by Ernest George and Harold Peto.

THE ARTS & CRAFTS ARCHITECTS

PHILIP SPEAKMAN WEBB (1831-1915)

Philip Webb was one of the most important early practitioners in the Arts and Crafts style. As a young man he served as Chief Clerk in the Office of George Edmund Street, the famous High Victorian Gothic architect and it was here that he met and became lifelong friends with one of the most influential thinkers of the century, William Morris. The two men were partners in the first Arts and Crafts business, Morris Marshall Faulkner & Co, set up to provide furnishings and fittings in the new style, and Webb designed The Red house at Upton in Kent for Morris in 1859 *(See Fig. 1)*. In common with his contemporary, George Devey, Webb shunned publicity, relying on personal introductions for his commissions, and it was by this method that he built up a very successful country house practice. Like Devey, Webb studied earlier building traditions and favoured using local materials. He wanted to make architecture the pursuit of honest building with great attention paid to detailing. Webb designed several houses in Surrey including Joldwynds in the wooded slopes above Holmbury St Mary, Willinghurst in the wooded slopes above Cranleigh and Coneyhurst in the woods above Ewhurst. His last house Hurlands, was built in 1896 near Guildford, this time near the foot of the Hog's Back. It is a brick house designed in a mixture of 'Queen Anne' with a French flavour. In this it represents a departure from the Arts and Crafts style but does adhere to the basic principle of using local materials with informality and comfort in the interior arrangements. The house was subdivided into four units in the 1950's.

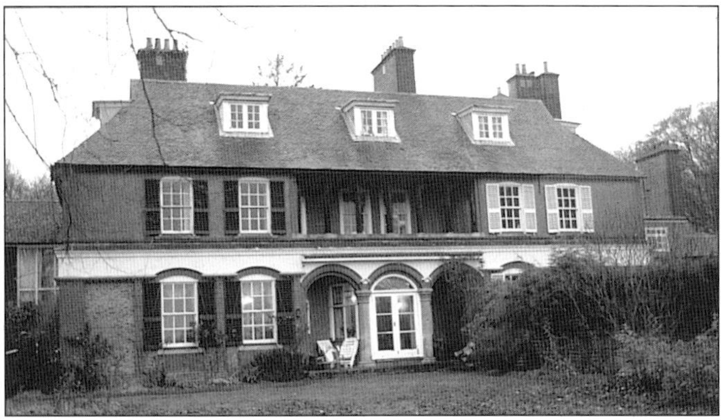

Fig. 12: Garden elevation of Hurlands (1896), Philip Webb's last country house.

EDWIN LUTYENS (1869-1944)

Later in his career, Lutyens' work departed from Arts and Crafts principles, but his early career in Surrey demonstrates how study of local buildings and craft techniques could inform and influence new design. It was the inspiration of the local buildings and picturesque countryside of south-west Surrey that led him to create some of his most sophisticated and attractive houses that became world famous. Sir Edwin Landseer Lutyens, the tenth child in a family of thirteen, was the son of Charles Lutyens, a retired army officer turned artist who had studied under Landseer, the famous Victorian artist. Family circumstances led to the Lutyens' moving down to Thursley in Surrey, where as a child, Edwin was free to explore the local countryside and study both the local buildings and traditions. In 1887, at the age of sixteen he enrolled on a two year architecture course at the Royal College of Art, although his interest remained with the local vernacular building traditions of Surrey. This interest was recorded by a neighbour, Mrs Ellinor Arbuthnot, of Upper House, Shamley Green, who arranged a meeting between the young Lutyens and Norman Shaw, a famous and highly successful architect. Lutyens explained to Shaw his "fixed principles" in which he believed that "anything built by man should harmonize with nature and be built of local materials". To this end he experimented with creating agricultural buildings of mud encased wattles on wooden piles and roofed in heather. The older established architect wryly commented that Lutyens might find his newly rich patrons more attracted to recreating replicas of something they had seen on their foreign travels and be less impressed with living in cowsheds. (3)

Following two years as a pupil in the office of Ernest

George and Harold Peto, Lutyens set up his own London practice in Gray's Inn Square at the age of twenty, largely on the strength of commissions from his Surrey friends. His earliest houses derive partly from Shaw's 'Old English Style' with half-timber and brick under tiled roofs, as at the gardener's cottage at Littleworth Cross designed for Harry Mangles, the famous rhododendron grower. *(See Fig IV Colour illustration Lutyens' design for a cottage at Littleworth Cross, near Guildford)*

He also demonstrated an early and deft use of the local Bargate stone in the Lodges at Park Hatch in Hascombe of 1889. Crooksbury House, his first major commission, was built of red brick and was commissioned for Harry Mangles' sister, Agnes Chapman. As Lutyens was beginning his career he was introduced to Gertrude Jekyll, who was to be an important influence on his later life. They met at Littleworth, introduced by Harry Mangles, where Lutyens had an opportunity to put his theories on agricultural buildings into practice by building a few simple sheds with log frames covered in rough timber boarding and with clay tiled roofs. *(See Colour illustrations Fig. V Lutyens' drawing of the Fowl House and Fig. VI Lutyens' Fowl House as built at Littleworth Cross).*

It was with Gertrude Jekyll that Lutyens was to develop the Munstead area near Godalming and find his new interpretations of traditional vernacular architecture matched by her re-interpretations of traditional gardens.

The first collaboration of the architect and gardener in Guildford was just outside Shalford at The Stables, attached to an earlier Victorian and eighteenth century house, Little Tangley. This half-timber and tile-hung building with its dovecote is now a private house and retains some fragments of the Jekyll garden. The pair returned to the area much later in 1904-7 when Gertrude Jekyll herself commissioned Lutyens to build a small house in Bramley that she intended to let. This speculative venture was therefore to be a demonstration that the Lutyens/Jekyll collaboration was also a commercial proposition. Millmead House is tucked away off a narrow lane and is an L-shaped building approached through the garden wall, the pedimented main door being framed in a picturesque manner by the arched gateway. It seems that Miss Jekyll added two small outbuildings in front of the statutory building line without approval and was summoned to appear before the authorities for a breach of the building bye-laws. Although the court did not insist on their removal and deemed the outbuildings a public improvement, Miss Jekyll was fined five pounds sterling "to show the public that bye-laws could not be broken with impunity." (4)

Sir Reginald Bray commissioned minor works from Lutyens in 1892, including a lych-gate at Shere Church and shops in Middle Street with oversailing, rendered upper floors and bold oak detailing. These are now converted to tea-rooms.

Later, in 1894 Bray commissioned Lutyens to build a lodge for the Manor House at Shere, and the architect produced a masterful compact composition of angled elements with a battered (or sloping) Bargate stone base and roughcast above.(5) *(See Fig I Colour illustration The Lodge in Shere)*

In 1894, Lutyens was commissioned by Miss Susan Muir Mackenzie, a good friend of Gertrude Jekyll, to design her house in Effingham, to be set in a Jekyll garden.

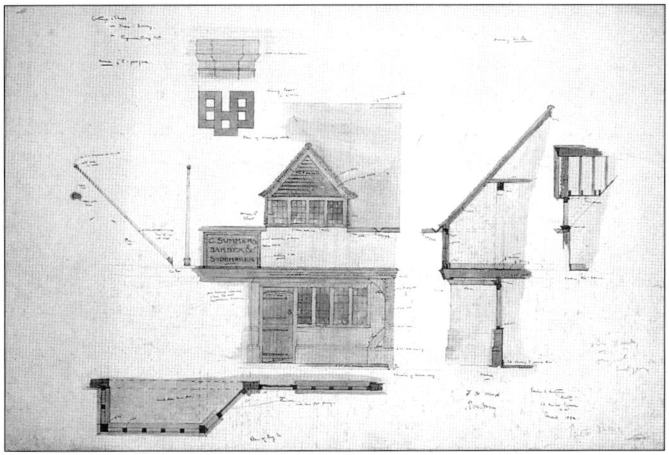

Fig 13: 1892 Drawing by Edwin Lutyens of a shop in Middle Street, Shere, for C. Summers, Barber and Shoemaker now converted into tea-rooms.
Courtesy of the British Architectural Library RIBA

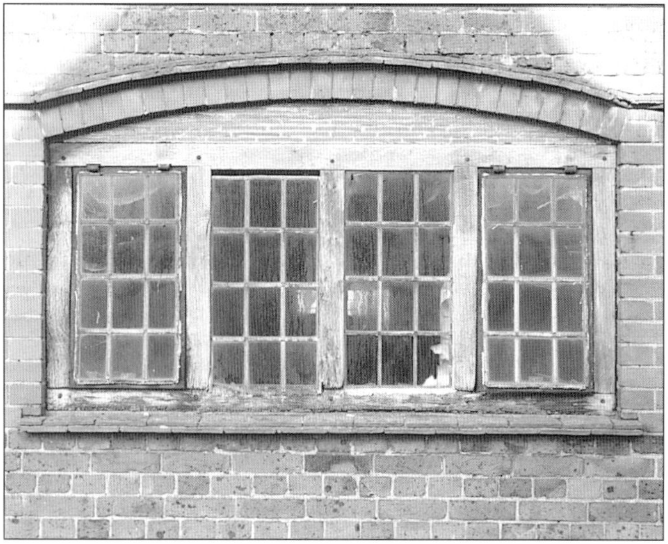

Fig. 14: Tympana detail above the window head on the Dairy at Cross Farm, Shackleford (1911) which is similar to the detail used by Lutyens at the Red House, Effingham.

Here at The Red house, Lutyens experimented with a formal Tudor design, although still using the local Bargate stone but with red brick dressings, and culminating in elegantly shaped brick copings on the parapets and gable ends. The Red House has several features that appear on later Lutyens' buildings, including the use of patterned tiles in the window tympana (the curved infill between the window lintel and the arch above) as well as the long horizontal bands of leaded casements. The windows on the front elevation have stone dressings and protruding tiles over their heads to provide protection from the rain. The roofline was simplified in 1955 but a tower-like wing to the right of the entrance has survived along with the massive brick chimney. The interior, although much changed in recent years, still has original timber boarded doors with wrought iron pull handles ending in heart shapes and the original balustrade to the stair with its comfortable wide handrails. The red paint inside the house which gave the building its name has

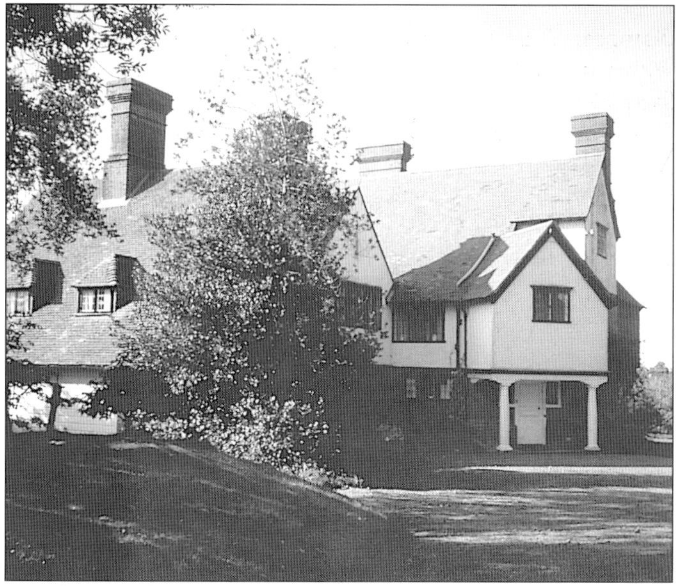

Fig. 15a: Lascombe (1894) by Edwin Lutyens. Entrance elevation

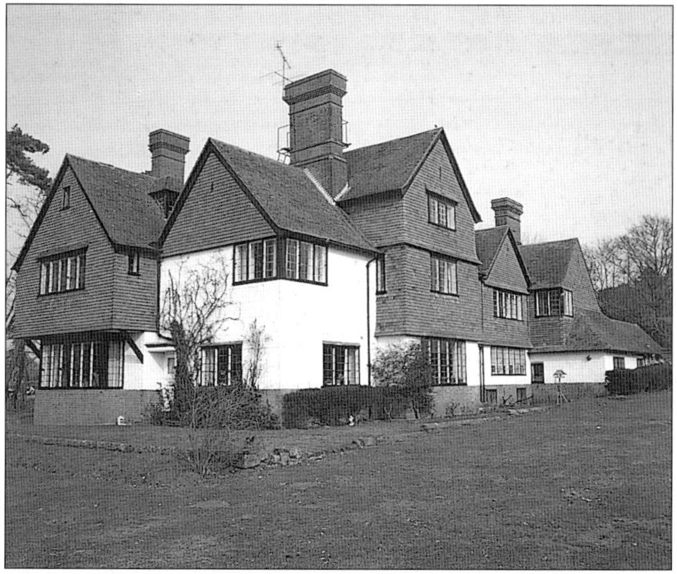

Fig. 15b: Lascombe (1894) by Edwin Lutyens. Garden elevation

disappeared, as has the Jekyll garden. Today the Red House, with many additions, is the home of the Convent of the Sacred Passion.

A third collaboration between Lutyens and Jekyll is Lascombe of 1894 at Puttenham. This is a comfortable family house in an informal Surrey cottage style with red brick to the ground floor and a combination of tile-hanging and render above, under a clay tile roof. The leaded casement fenestration includes the occasional corner window and in the forecourt the entrance porch is tucked diagonally into the corner and leads into an interestingly shaped entrance hall. Internally there are still many features surviving including the dark stained oak woodwork and an original fireplace surround in the hall. All of the major living rooms on the ground floor and the first floor bedrooms open onto the spacious staircase hall with its generous handrail and balustrades. A detail Lutyens obviously enjoyed devising was the cornice moulding that incorporates a picture rail, a sophisticated feature in an otherwise deceptively simple interior. The original Jekyll garden that complemented the house now no longer exists.

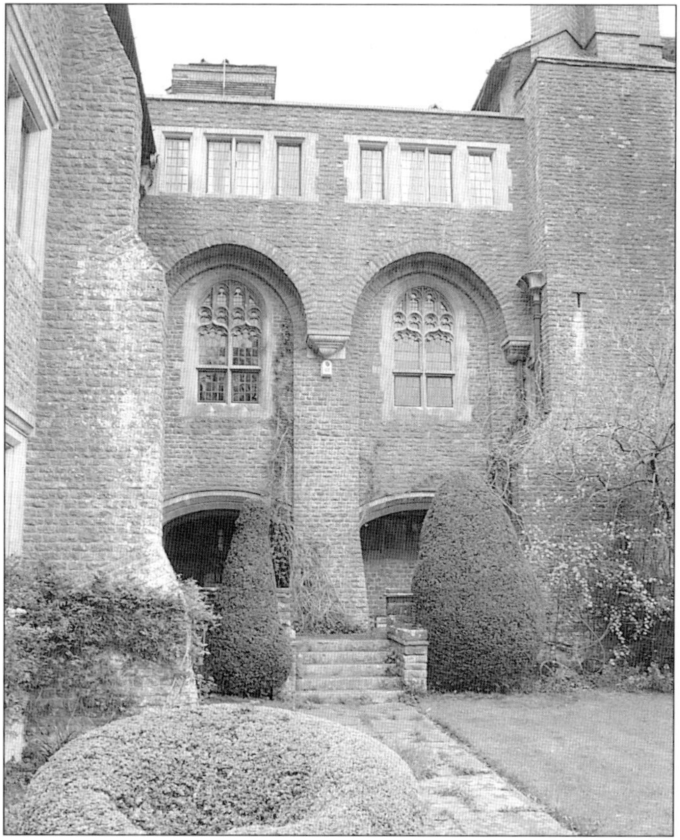

Fig. 16: Garden elevation of Chinthurst Hill with its Tudor windows (1894)

During the construction of Lascombe, Jekyll and Lutyens were conferring about a major country house commission from Miss Amelia Guthrie in 1893 at Chinthurst Hill, (straddling Guildford and the neighbouring Borough of Waverley). The architect and gardener must have thoroughly walked the extensive grounds before selecting the location near the summit of the hill for what was to be a dramatic, fortress-like house. The best southerly views were from the living rooms overlooking the Wey valley, and the house is situated at the end of a serpentine drive that winds up the side of the hill for a third of a mile before it reaches the entrance. Both architect and gardener concurred in principle that entrances to houses should be understated and the entrance to Chinthurst Hill is through a heavy oak door, modestly placed. The Bargate stone blocks of the main house are left with a rustic finish, with smooth ashlar dressings to windows and arches. The horizontal rhythm of the house is continued by the ranges of windows, counterbalanced by the great stone chimneys and Tudor arches, Internally, a dramatic main hall with massive timber beams and its adjacent staircase continue the Tudor flavour, whilst the first storey corridor with its simple white plastered arches is a foretaste of Lutyens' later interiors. The spectacular views across the site are not visible until reaching the wide terrace planned by Miss Jekyll which was to be planted with double herbaceous beds and a grey border. The house was subdivided in the 1950's but much of the original garden has survived. *(See Fig VII Colour illustration – View from Chinthurst Hill)*

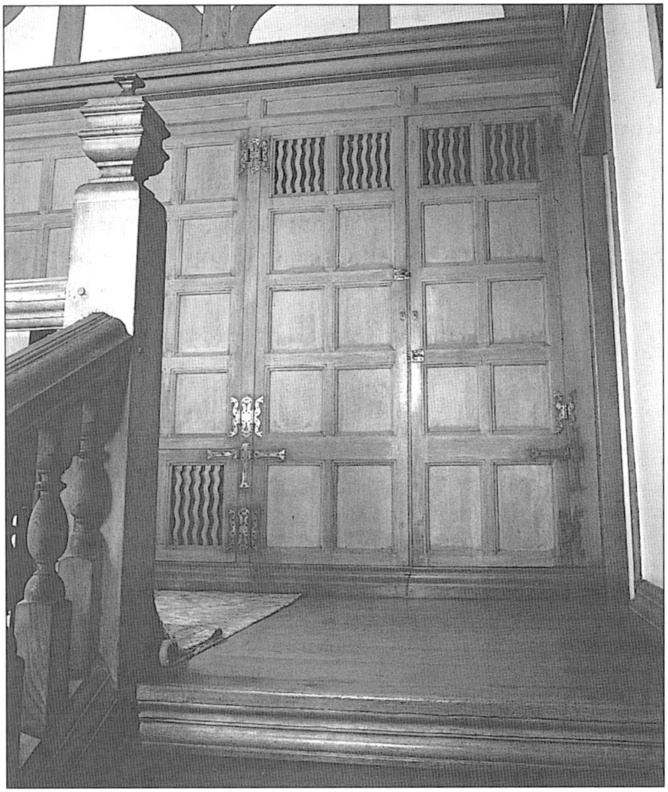

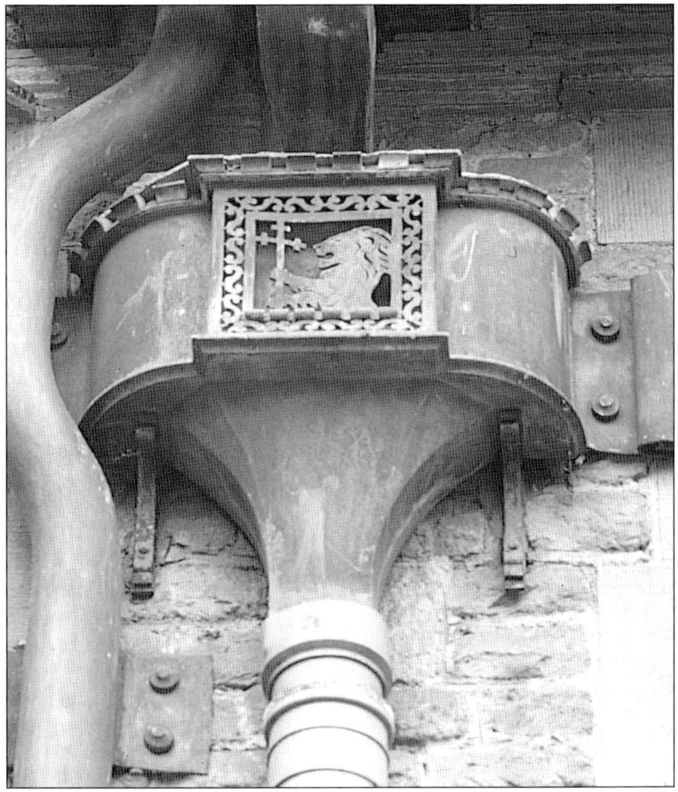

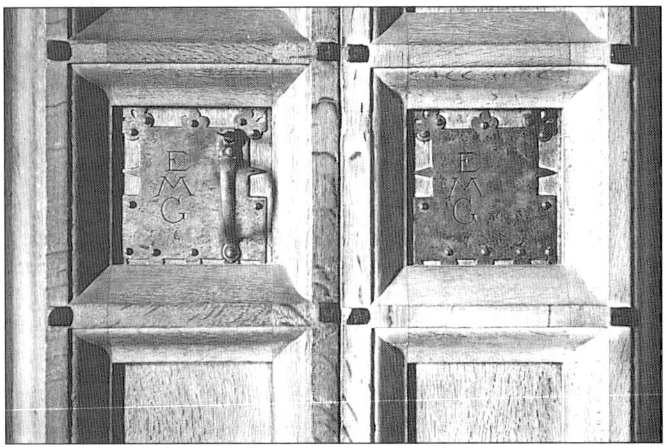

Top Left: Fig. 17a: First floor landing at Chinthurst Hill. Note quality of joinery and swan-neck hinges to the door.

Above: Fig. 17b: Lead rainwater hopper head at Chinthurst Hill

Left: Fig. 17c: Detail of Oak door furniture to the hall at Chinthurst Hill

In 1899 Littlecroft, Lutyens' last house in Guildford, was completed in the Guildown area. This compact house is built on a steeply sloping site and utilizes a clever split level plan to take advantage of the contours. The front elevation, hard up to the pavement appears to be single storey and contains a simple arched brick entrance. The entrance is into a compact hall with a top-lit stairwell in a relaxed classical style. The main living rooms are half a flight down, whilst the bedrooms are half a flight up in a symmetrical plan with all of the rooms opening off the hall. The simple interior design includes panelled doors, picture rails at door head height and wide simple flat balusters to the staircase. The rear elevation reflects the symmetrical plan with two bay windows flanking the central doors from the hall into the garden.

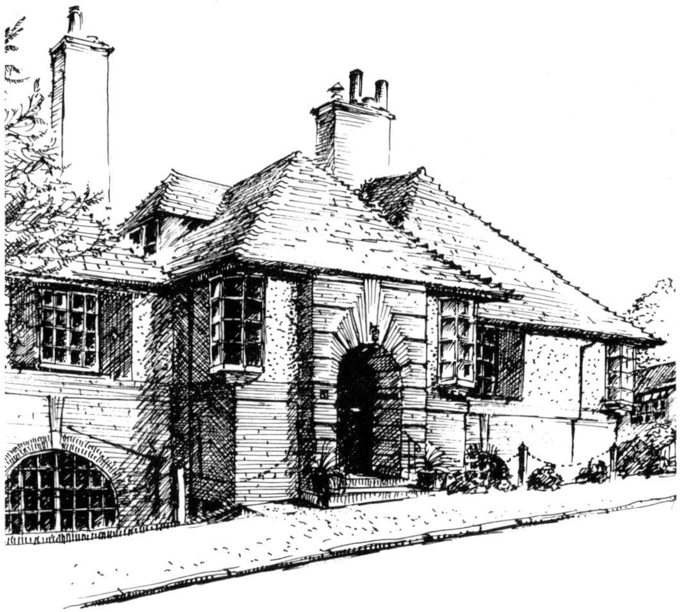

Fig. 18: Sketch of street elevation of Littlecroft (1899), one of Lutyens' smaller houses and his last major commission in Guildford.

Although Lutyens was already using different styles for his early houses he was consistent in his design approach for his buildings which all presented a modest face to the world, and reserved the drama for the garden side of the house where it would often be complemented by the planting and garden designs of Gertrude Jekyll, extending the house into the wider landscape. The greatest examples of this partnership at work in this fashion are to be found in the developments at Munstead, and particularly Munstead Wood, which was built in 1896 by Lutyens on land Miss Jekyll had purchased opposite her mother's home near Godalming. The design of the Bargate stone house was the result of a mutually creative working relationship between client and architect. The deceptively simple stone facades contain oak framed casement windows of traditional character under a tiled roof that extends down towards the ground floor, making the building appear to grow out of its site. The drama unfolds in the half-timbered, jettied gallery that overhangs the northern courtyard leading to the ponds and steps laid out by Jekyll. The house is no longer simply a Classical or Tudor derived design but a re-interpretation of many of the features found in local vernacular buildings in a disciplined form. As Gertrude Jekyll wrote:

> *"... the architect has a thorough knowledge of the local ways of using the sandstone that grows in our hills, and that for many centuries has been the building material of the district, and of all the lesser incidental methods of adapting means to ends that mark the well defined way of building of the country, so that what he builds seems to grow naturally out of the ground...I hold as a convincing canon of architecture that every building should look like what it is..."*(6)

Lutyens' career spanned the world but soon after his early projects around Guildford he turned from Arts and Crafts style to a more formal Classical approach. The Jekyll/Lutyens partnership survived the stylistic changes and flourished until she died in 1932, producing more than 100 collaborations between gardener and architect.

C.F.A. VOYSEY (1857-1941)

One of the most uncompromising architects of the period, often labelled Arts and Crafts, but a label he vigorously denied, was Charles Francis Annesley Voysey.

Born in Hessle, Yorkshire, he attended his father's school as a child until his father was forced to move the family to Dulwich in 1871, following a theological dispute, where he founded the Theistic Church. In 1873 Voysey was articled to the Victorian architect J.P. Seddon when he was made aware of the writings of Ruskin. Voysey moved to George Devey's practice in 1880 where the latter's design for the St Alban's Court Estate appears to have influenced his early works; certainly Voysey employed similar horizontality and long bands of windows placed hard up under the eaves to that used by Devey in this estate. He started his own practice in 1882, supporting himself on refurbishment work and wallpaper, fabric and furniture designs. As a result of the publication of his ideal country house design in 1889 in "British Architect" his practice prospered.

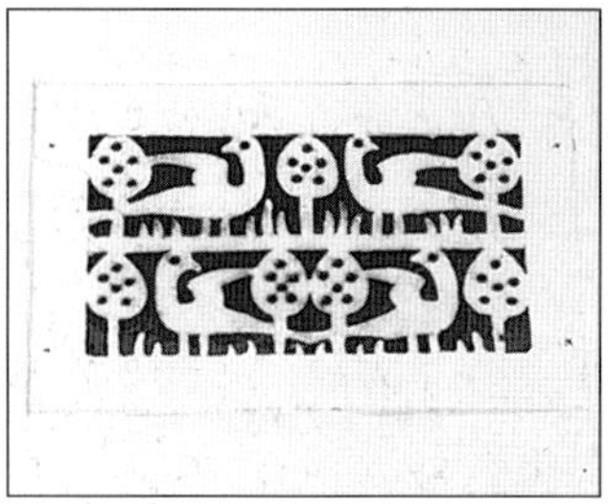

Fig. 19a Typical Voysey ventilation grille to chimney, used in many of his houses.

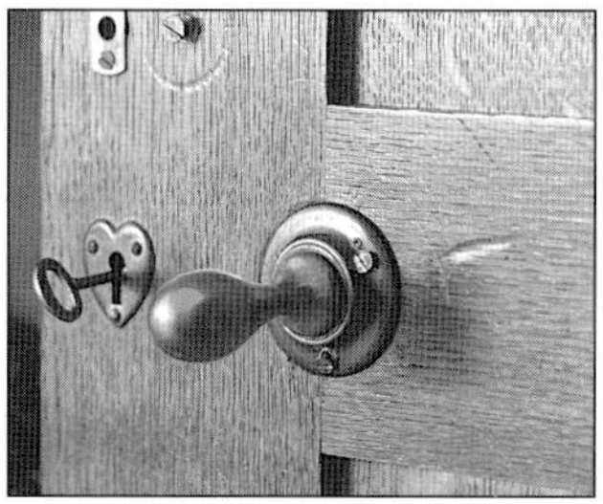

Fig. 19b Door furniture at Priorsfield showing heart-shaped escutcheon

In his choice of plain roughcast for his facades, largely irrespective of their geographical location, Voysey went against the idea of using local materials, a principle fundamental to Arts and Crafts philosophy. His use of roughcast applied over nine inch brickwork is explained as an economic and weathertight alternative to thicker, more expensive masonry walls. His use of buttresses was also an economic measure permitting thinner wall construction between them, as well as adding a three dimensional rhythm to facades and creating small private spaces for occasional garden furniture. Voysey also adopted the long, thin Arts and Crafts plan of one room and a corridor in width; he placed servants' quarters upstairs in light and airy spaces stating that "*...cheap and nasty treatment of servants will be regarded as dishonouring to the master*".(7) Voysey's humanity stems from a personal morality since he did not share an enthusiasm for socialism which other Arts and Crafts practitioners promulgated.

Voysey's approach to interior design called for lower rooms with ceilings about eight feet high which he felt could be heated economically and lit naturally with lower windows. He delighted in designing personal details for his houses such as heart-shaped letter plates, bird shaped patterns on his ventilation grilles and even iron brackets shaped in his client's profiles. This concern with the personal, handcrafted or designed fittings throughout the building is central to an Arts and Crafts approach. However, unlike the orthodox Arts and Crafts theorists, Voysey accepted the machine as a useful tool as can be seen by his use of selected manufactured items in many of his houses, including downpipe brackets and some of the ventilation grilles.

Guildford has four major Voysey houses and his fully mature style is demonstrated in the Sturgis house of 1896, on the Hog's Back above Puttenham, now renamed Greyfriars. Additions built for Sturgis's son in 1913 unfortunately obliterated the original roofline at the west end which featured green-grey Westmoreland Slates sweeping down on a steep pitch to low eaves at the ground floor, a feature much used by Arts and Crafts architects in other materials. (8) The roughcast finish contrasts with the smooth ashlar around the leaded casement windows and the boldly projecting bay windows. A wide, low oak entrance door has typical wrought iron door furniture and due to the long narrow site the house is approached at its side, with the main entrance on the long rear elevation. The principal garden elevation with its elegant double height bay windows and long central verandah faces the fine southern views, whilst a wrought iron gate at the far west end leads to generously proportioned flights of stone stairs that wind gently down to a clearing containing tennis courts and timber summer houses in the valley below the house. The investment in literally hundreds of feet of stone paving and steps is indicative of the wealth of some of the late Victorians and, conversely, the meagre day wages paid to skilled labourers who built their country retreats.

In 1897 Voysey designed Norney Grange, a substantial house with an extremely attractive and picturesque lodge for the Reverend Leighton Grane, an artistically inclined clergyman. The house was set in extensive grounds that remain largely intact and contained summer-houses and a garden designed by the architect. Stables were added in 1903. Externally, Norney bears many trademarks of the architect including roughcast walls with simple buttressing, slate roofs, deep projecting eaves, bands of leaded casement windows in smooth stone dressings and distinctive chimneys. Voysey diverges from his standard approach, however, by experimenting with circular elements in the design, most noticeably in the asymmetrically placed classical entrance porch with its large round window and semi-circular gable above the main door, resulting in an atypically prominent front entrance. The semi-circular gable is repeated on the side elevations and also internally in the oak-panelled entrance hall, with the theme repeated in the semi-circular

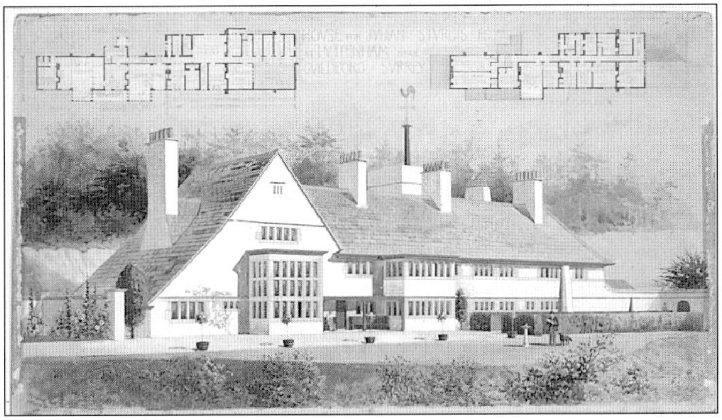

Fig. 20: *Voysey's presentation plan and garden elevation of Sturgis House (now Greyfriars)* Courtesy of the British Architectural Library, RIBA

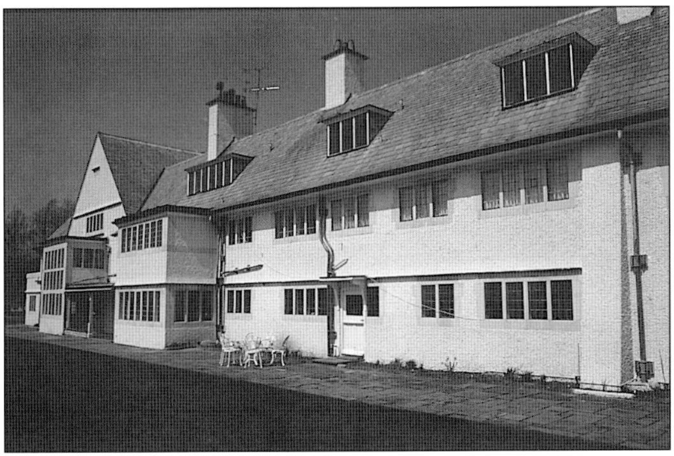

Fig. 21: *Garden elevation of Greyfriars today.* Photograph Courtesy Surrey County Council

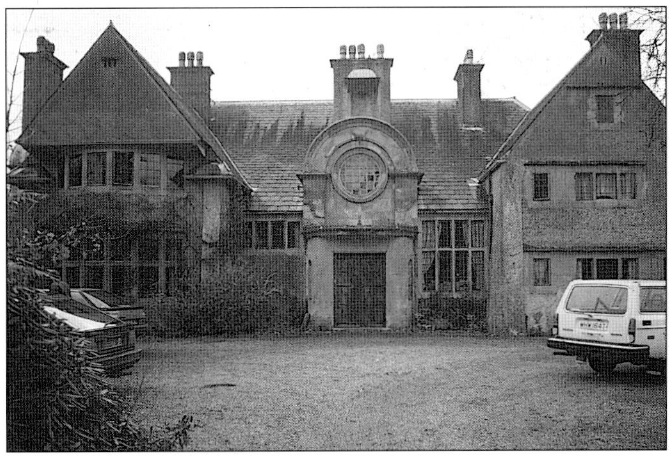

Fig 22 Entrance elevation to Norney Grange (1897) by C F A Voysey.

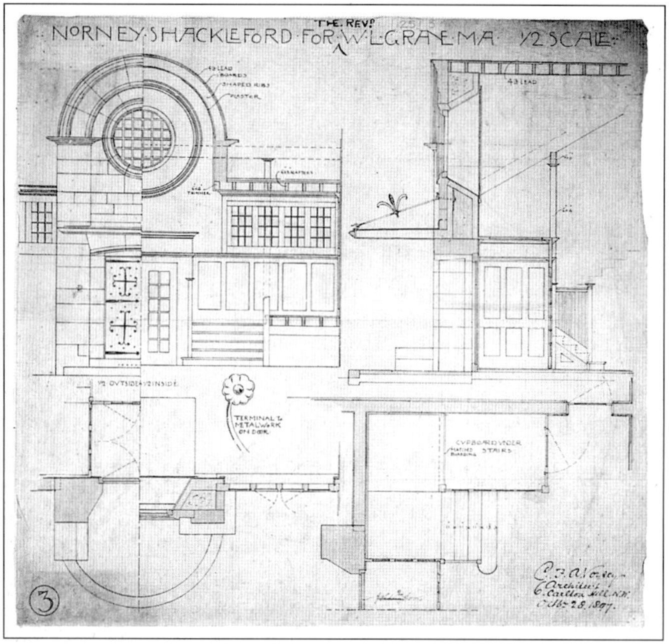

Fig 23 *Voysey's working drawing of entrance to Norney Grange (1897).* Courtesy of British Architectural Library RIBA
(See Fig VIII Colour illustration Presentation drawings by C F A Voysey of entrance and garden elevations of Norney Grange).

projections to the first floor gallery. The simple stick balustrade of the staircase complements the very sophisticated use of space in the hall which is the central circulation area of the house. Norney retains many of its original internal features and handcrafted ironmongery designed by Voysey.

Prior's Field, was a moderately sized house between Puttenham and Compton designed by Voysey for Mr F. H. Chambers in 1900. Chambers never occupied the house and in 1901 Mr and Mrs Leonard Huxley bought it and obtained permission from the local authority to establish a "High Class School for Girls" on the premises. Leonard Huxley was a master at nearby Charterhouse and his wife Julia became the headmistress of the new school, welcoming her first pupils in January 1902 – comprising one boarder and five day girls. Numbers were made up by her seven year old son Aldous, who remained the lone boy at Prior's Field for several years. Julia Huxley, who was the niece of the poet Matthew Arnold and granddaughter of Dr Arnold of Rugby, and her husband Leonard, son of scientist Thomas Henry Huxley, both had progressive ideas about the education of girls. The new school was committed to providing a well-

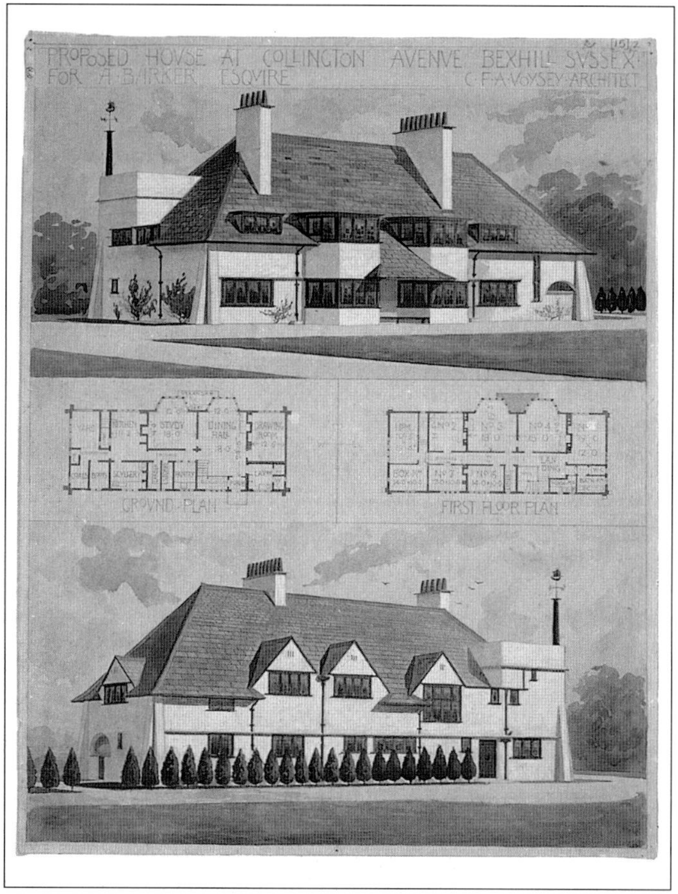

Fig 24 *Voysey's design for house at Bexhill, Sussex, (1898) which was never built. The same design was used at Priors Garth (now Priors Field)* Courtesy of British Architectural Library RIBA

rounded education in the Arts, Sciences and Physical Training coupled with certain freedoms – freedom of choice, freedom of expression and freedom to refrain from attending church, with parental permission. The alternative to religious worship was attending readings of Plato's "Dialogues".

The school was immediately popular, which attests to the presence of intellectually adventurous patrons, and by 1904 had 43 boarders and six day girls. The increase in numbers meant that new additions were required and these were designed by Thomas Muntzer, Voysey's pupil. The 1904 additions clearly modified the original house. However, research by a teacher at the school revealed that the house was built to designs dating from 1898 for a house in Bexhill, Sussex, which was never built. The importance of the Bexhill design is that it was conceived concurrently with

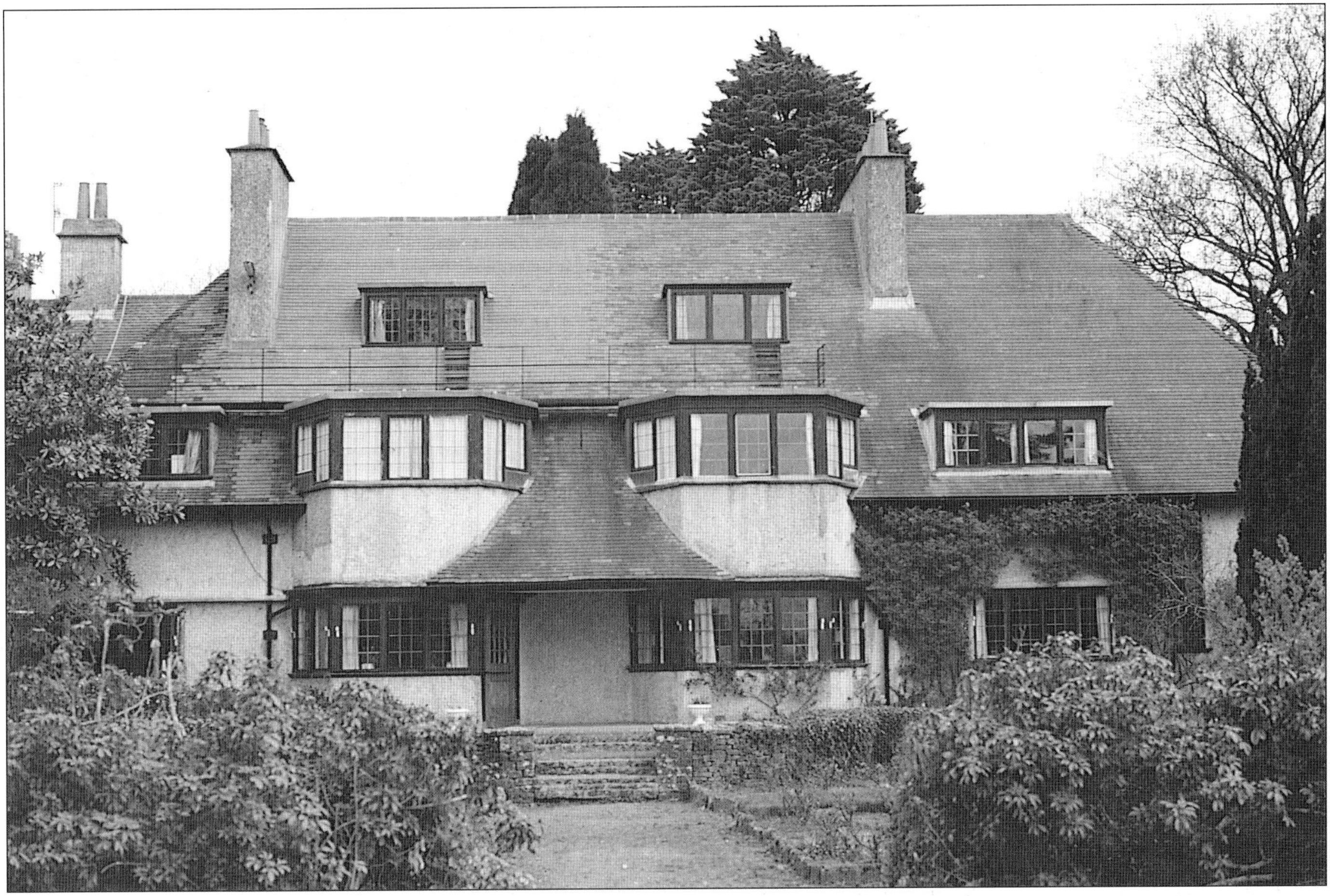

Fig 25 Garden elevation of Priors Field School today.

Voysey's two most admired houses, Broadleys and Moor Crag, both also dating from 1898 and both in the Lake District. (9) Internally, the school retains many original features, a fine oak hall and staircase, original fireplaces and ironmongery on the doors and some windows. The Muntzer additions endeavoured to maintain Voysey's themes; his gymnasium built in 1906 has dramatic crown-post roof trusses. The garden plan was provided by the architect but the planting scheme was devised by Leonard Huxley in consultation with Gertrude Jekyll, some of which still exists.

Voysey's final house in Guildford is Littleholme in the Guildown area built in 1907 by and for the builder George Muntzer. It features the familiar roughcast, limestone ashlar dressings to the windows and doors and long runs of leaded casements. His entrance elevation with its wide oak door is understated as usual and his more complex garden elevation with its two storey bay windows, opens onto the terraced garden on a sloping site, with fine views bounded by yew hedges. The house was subdivided into four units in the 1950's. *(See Fig IX Colour illustration; wide, round headed oak door at Littleholme, by Voysey.)*

After the First World War, Voysey's architectural practice, which had produced over a hundred private houses as well as a factory for the wallpaper firm of Sanderson and Sons, had diminished into obscurity. Unlike many of his contemporaries, who were willing to design in any style the client wanted, Voysey was adamant in maintaining his artistic integrity and did not want to be categorized as a follower of any particular design approach. Once he stated his principles he did not deviate from them. His interiors were based on practical ideas developed early in his career and his buildings today are viewed as a bridge between the Arts and Crafts and the Modern Movement in architecture. In his own words, he believed wholeheartedly that:

> *"Simplicity, repose, directness and frankness are moral qualities as essential to good architecture as to good men..."* (10)

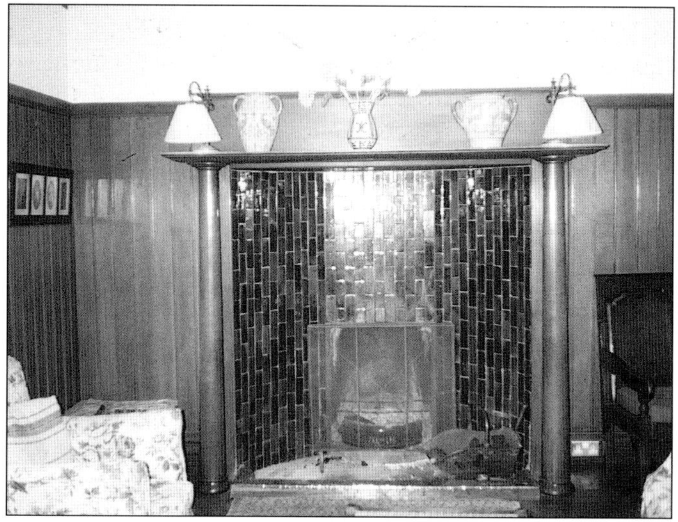

Fig. 26a Fireplace in the Oak Room at Priors Field, with green tiling probably made at Wrecclesham Pottery, Farnham.

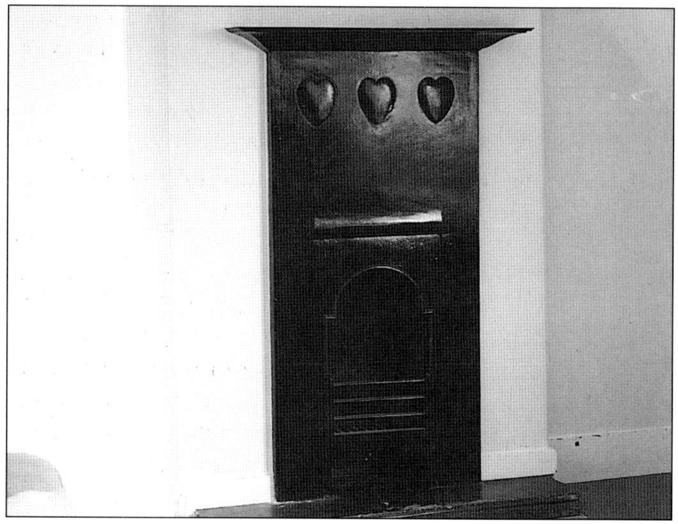

Fig. 26b Simple cast-iron dormitory fireplace at Priors Field with typical Voysey heart motifs.

HUGH THACKERAY TURNER (1850-1937)

Although not internationally renowned, Thackeray Turner is an important architect committed to Arts and Crafts principles whose Guildford work was much admired by the late architectural historian Nikolaus Pevsner.

In his best buildings, Thackeray Turner's designs are completely straightforward, with no overt historic references. Turner was articled to Sir George Gilbert Scott (1811-1878) one of the most influential architects of the High Victorian Gothic Revival and, in 1877, whilst serving his apprenticeship he became Secretary of the newly formed Society for the Protection of Ancient Buildings (SPAB), a post he held for 29 years.

Nicknamed "anti-scrape", the Society vehemently opposed the refacing of old stonework and the thorough, although sometimes unresearched restorations of Medieval buildings that was so prevalent in Victorian England. Founded by William Morris, Philip Webb and other like-minded architects, the Society also became an informal school for exchanging information on traditional construction techniques since meetings tended to end in long discussions on the subject at Gatti's restaurant in the Strand.

Thackeray Turner married a Guildford girl in 1888, the daughter of Thomas Wilde Powell of Piccards Rough, but he had a London based practice in partnership with Eustace Balfour, and ongoing work as architects to the Grosvenor Estate in Mayfair. It was not until 1899 that he moved into Surrey, when he built his own home, Westbrook, near Godalming. However, his earliest work in Guildford, The Wycliffe Buildings, dates from 1894.

The Wycliffe Buildings were commissioned as an experiment in social housing by Thomas Wilde Powell, Thackeray Turner's father-in-law, who immediately bequeathed it upon completion to a charitable trust presided over by the Minister of the Congregational Church in Guildford and other trustees of Nonconformist beliefs. According to the Trust deeds of 9th September 1895:

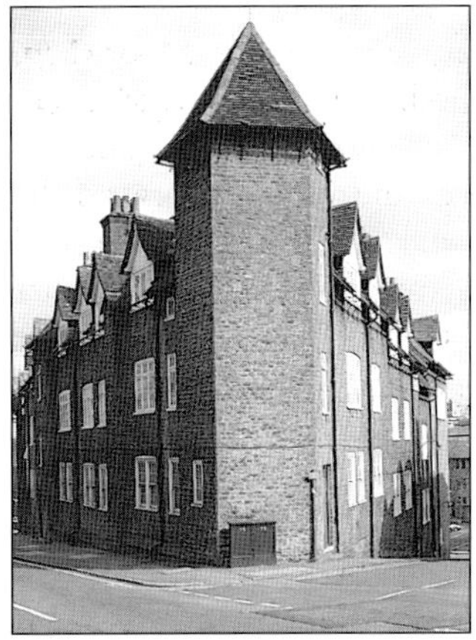

Fig. 27a *Wycliffe Buildings*, (1894) by Thackeray Turner, Portsmouth Road Guildford.

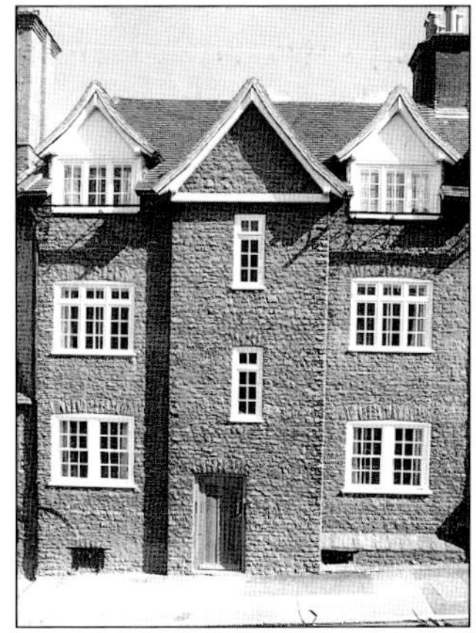

Fig. 27b *Wycliffe Buildings*: view of entrance frontage on Portsmouth Road.

> *"...The tenements had to be let to such persons approved by the Trustees at a fair and moderate rent, but preference to be given to abstainers from alcoholic liquors..."* (11)

The Wycliffe Buildings Trust administered the building for over one hundred years. Recently renovated by a housing association, it remains in multiple occupancy. This three storey building of coursed Bargate stone has a tower to anchor it visually at the top of its sloping site. It has no consciously historic detailing, but relies on the pattern of fenestration and gables to provide interest, particularly on the side elevations which rise abruptly from the street.

Internally, sinuous timber handrails follow the spiral stairs with their central wooden newel, whilst in the attic room of the building are the remains of the communal laundry. It was greatly admired by Pevsner who praised it for its "humanity and friendliness". He stated that:

> *"....it is quite the best of its kind in the country, beautifully adapted to an awkward, wedge-shaped sloping site, with all the subtle play of gables and eaves that the LCC (London County Council) used a little later..."* (12)

Thackeray Turner also designed Mead Cottage, a tiny L-shaped Bargate stone house in the nearby Buryfields with similar lack of historic references, its effect relying on the materials and the only overt piece of decoration being the use of curving wrought iron brackets to support the gutters, which he also used on the Wycliffe Buildings.

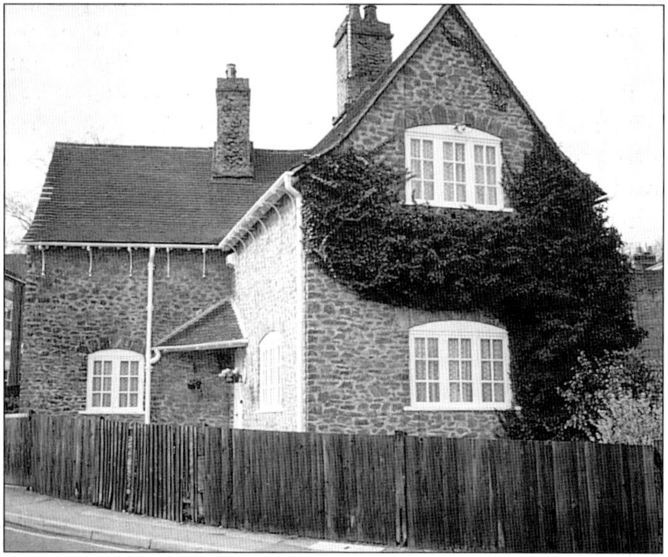

Fig. 28: Mead Cottage, (1895) by Thackeray Turner.

With the Secretary of the SPAB at work in the town, it must have been no surprise to Guildford's Remembrancer, Dr. George Williamson, to receive a letter from SPAB in 1896 expressing concern about the future of Guildford's High Street and urging residents to form a "watching committee". Dr. Williamson called a public meeting which was held in the Borough Hall in North Street on 3rd November 1896. Among the comments was a written statement from William Morris emphasizing the dangers threatening the town's unique High Street. The meeting resolved to establish a civic protection society to be known as The Old Guildford Society.(13) Thackeray Turner never joined the committee, but a later recruit was Edwin Lutyens. The Old Guildford Society only lasted six years, during which time it managed to save Guildford Old Bank (1765), now well preserved as Lloyds Bank in the High Street. The Society would not then be revived until 1935.

Thackeray Turner's final building in Guildford is another experiment in multiple occupancy, also in the Buryfields area, The Court of 1902. This U-shaped building contains fifteen terraced houses embracing a shared green. The three storey design, incorporating dormers, makes use of simple detailing with brick and render elevations under a tiled roof and tall brick chimneys adding vertical interest. The floors are constructed of eleven inch thick concrete, running in continuous slabs at both first and second floors. At the second floor, the slab protrudes outside the building to form a generous eaves. Today, the use of concrete floors is the standard way to achieve fire-resistant separation between floors, but in Turner's day it was by no means the norm. Experimentation with concrete technology had been discussed at length in the architectural press in the 1860's and 1870's with concrete foundations used for the first time in 1845, followed by concrete floors in 1865. Even Arts and Crafts architects committed to the use of traditional materials saw a place for concrete technology, most famously at Brockhampton Church, Herefordshire by W. R. Lethaby.

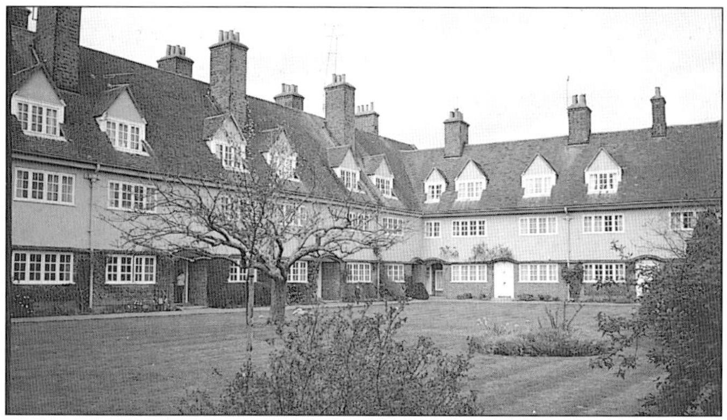

Fig. 29: The Court, (1902), Buryfields by Thackeray Turner. A typical example of garden suburb housing, as found notably in Hampstead Garden Suburb.

MACKAY HUGH BAILLIE SCOTT (1865-1945)

Baillie Scott, a contemporary of Lutyens, Voysey and Thackeray Turner was deeply committed to craftsmanship in architecture. Although trained in agriculture in order to run the family sheep farm in Australia, he changed profession to that of architect and practised in England, first on the Isle of Man and later in Bedford. In 1894 the publication of his design for an ideal house in "The Studio" a leading arts journal, led to his earliest commissions both in England and on the Continent. The published design was a simple version of the preferred Arts and Craft plan of one room and a corridor in width. Within such simple plans Scott created varied and dramatic interiors and developed his re-creation of a great hall for living, complete with minstrels' gallery and inglenook, features which brought him repeat commissions. In 1904, in his seminal study of the English Arts and Crafts Movement "Das Englische Haus", which introduced the German public to the innovative developments in English architecture, Hermann Muthesius wrote of Baillie Scott that he was the first architect "to have realized the interior as an autonomous work of art". These comments brought commissions for elaborate interiors for the Grand Duke of Hesse at Darmstadt, Grand Duke Ernst Ludwig and several mansions in Germany. His houses for English clients were less grand and more influenced by Voysey's work, which he stated "consists mainly in the application of severely sane, practical and rational ideas to home making". (14)

Baillie Scott's prolific career includes three houses on the south side of Guildford, all dating from between 1910-1913. Undershaw (1910) was designed on six different levels in order to take advantage of the steeply sloping site. Constructed of local materials in the Arts and Crafts manner the house is entered by way of a dramatic pergola on chunky stone columns, (*see front cover*). Baillie Scott's talent for interior design is amply demonstrated in his handling of the two major rooms, the formal drawing room, with its delicately moulded white plaster walls being in contrast to the Tudor-style oak panelled Hall complete with gallery, showing the range of sources he drew upon. Garden Court (1913) is similar to Undershaw in its external appearance and has a large garden designed by Gertrude Jekyll. However, with Monks Path in 1912, Scott departs from Arts and Crafts principles and designs this house in a Neo-Georgian style, an uncharacteristic decision for the architect who remained an advocate of the Arts and Crafts approach throughout his career. However, a change of taste to a more formal style for houses became widespread in England just prior to the Great War for a variety of reasons, including a growing preference for regular buildings. The vernacular Arts and Crafts approach had never been popular for civic buildings in towns and cities, as it had always been considered too informal. Architects who wished to keep the commissions flowing found that they were obliged to offer Classical designs, or designs in an 'appropriate' style, if they were not to face a diminishing number of projects.

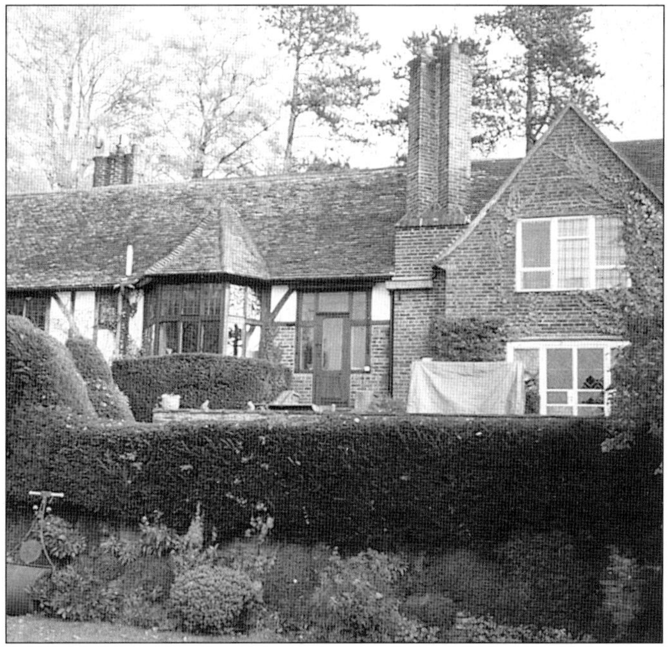

Fig 30 *A Guildford house by Baillie Scott in the Arts and Crafts Style.*

THE WATTS IN COMPTON

A short train ride from the world's greatest financial capital opened up the leisurely world of rural village life with its attractive cottages, pretty wild flowers and picturesque rolling countryside. This marvellous backdrop, within easy reach of Guildford's main line station was being discovered by the new artistic elite. George Bernard Shaw was known to have spent time at Piccard's Cottage from 1900 to 1902 and J.M. Barrie was so enchanted with Shere that he was a regular visitor with his personally selected cricket team from London to challenge the locals on the village green. Among the enlightened City gents who put down roots in the area was Andrew Hitchens, President of the Stock Exchange and frequent host to Mary and George Frederic Watts.

G.F. Watts (1817-1904) was already a much admired painter of allegorical themes in the 1840's, before most of the well known Arts and Crafts architects were born. A favourite of the intelligentsia, he spent twenty five years as a guest of Mr. and Mrs Thoby Prinsep at Little Holland House, one of the great Victorian 'Salons' frequented by Tennyson, Ruskin, Burne-Jones, Thackeray and the artistically inclined nobility. It was here that the painter was introduced to Ellen Terry, a striking young actress whom he married in 1864, just before her seventeenth birthday and his forty-seventh. The bride was impulsive and high-spirited, the groom pampered and self-centred; clearly the marriage was doomed to failure. Encouraged by his friends, Watts separated from Ellen in 1865 but it was to take a further ten years before they divorced. Although Watts met his second wife-to-be, Mary Fraser-Tytler in 1870, it took her sixteen determined years to coax him into matrimony again, in his sixty-ninth year and her thirty-sixth. Mary devoted herself completely to her 'Signor' and set about making him into a legend in his lifetime. Fearful that the London fogs were detrimental to his health and delighted by their visits to the Hitchens at Monkshatch, the Watts decided to build their winter home "Limnerslease" on a charming wooded site near Compton. Their chosen architect was Sir Ernest George who provided two studios and ample servants quarters, but unfortunately omitted a staircase from the first to the second floors – or so the story goes!

Their winter house was a great success and the couple moved permanently to Compton where Watts spent the last thirteen years of his life painting and sculpting prolifically, whilst Mary attended to his every need. Her secondary interest was in supporting the Home Arts and Industries Association, an organization founded in the mid 1880's dedicated to the revival of village handicrafts as a means of providing skilled work for the rural poor, ideals which were central to the social themes advanced by the Arts and Crafts Movement. Mary decided that Compton's craft would be pottery, following the discovery of an excellent bed of clay in the grounds of Limnerslease. When Compton Parish Council purchased a new plot of ground for village burials in 1895, the Watts enthusiastically offered the village the gift of a new mortuary chapel to be designed by Mary and decorated under her direction employing the unskilled villagers as labourers and craftsmen. In 1896, a kiln was set up at Limnerslease and evening pottery classes were started for the production of terracotta tiles to decorate the exterior of her unique Romanesque style chapel.

The ground plan formed of a "circle signifying Eternity cut by the Cross of Faith" translated itself into an extremely powerful physical presence. It is built of thin 'Roman' bricks with bands of Mary's handmade terracotta tiles richly decorated with Celtic symbolism. Although the chapel was dedicated by the Bishop of Winchester in July 1898, Mary did not decorate the domed interior until 1901, again aided by the village amateurs. Laden with symbolism, the interior is completely covered with stylized angels and cherubs' heads with sinuous Art Nouveau decoration depicting the Tree of Life. The whole is executed in gesso, i.e. fibre soaked in Plaster of Paris, and the chapel must be considered a unique monument, particularly as Mary had no formal architectural training and she was assisted by unskilled labour.

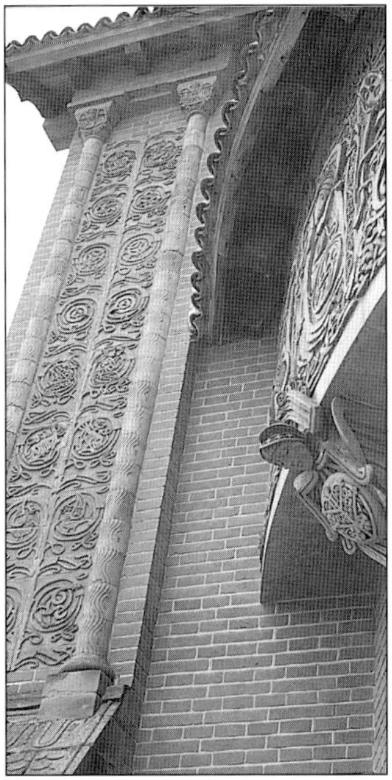

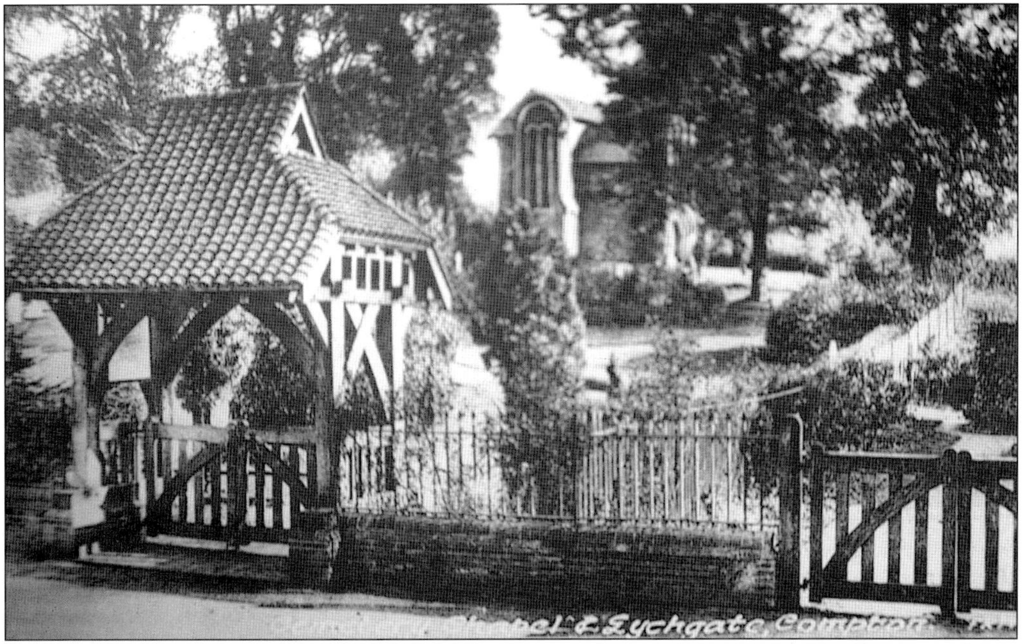

Top Right: Fig. 31: Photograph of Watts cemetery Chapel and Lych-gate.(1898) Courtesy of R. H. Jefferies. (Watts Gallery)

Above: Fig. 32: Watts Chapel exterior: detail of terracotta tiles, produced by Compton villagers. Courtesy Nigel Barker

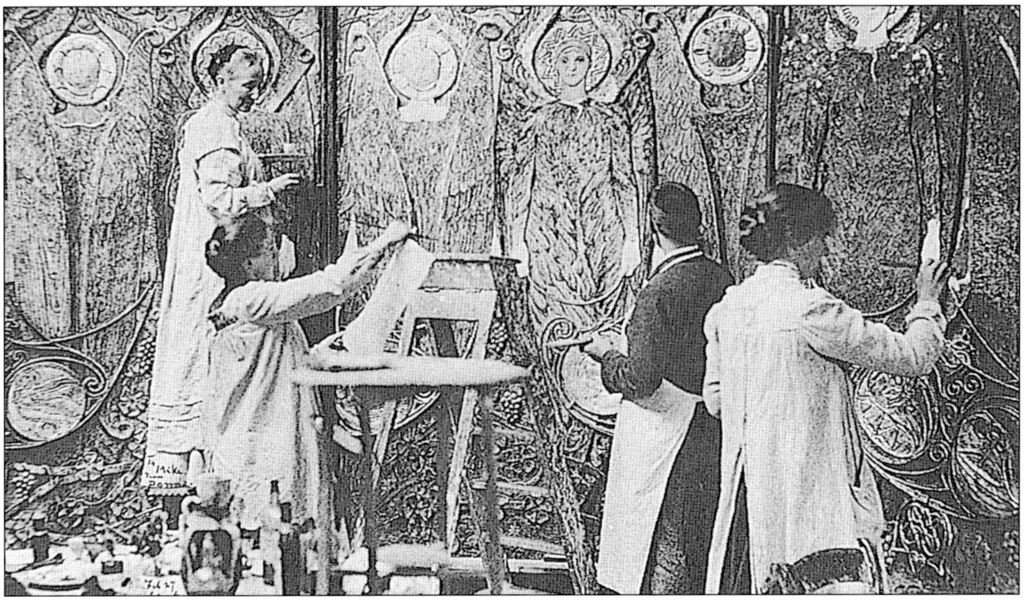

Right: Fig. 33: Mrs Watts working on the decoration for the Watts Chapel, (February 1906). Courtesy of the Watts Gallery.
(See Fig. XI Colour illustration: Watts Chapel interior gesso decoration depicting the Tree of Life, by Mary Watts and villagers)

Mary Watts continued her enterprising pottery by founding the Compton Potters Art Guild in 1902. The success of her pottery business meant that accommodation was needed for her young workers so she undertook a project that was dear to her heart – a purpose built gallery within view of Limnerslease for displaying her husband's paintings, with a hostel attached for her young potters. Designed by Christopher Turnor, who had worked for Lutyens but was not a professional architect, the gallery with its roughcast walls and red clay roof tiles was built in little over a year. Watts himself died in July 1904, just two months after the completion of the new building and his death was reported in newspapers all over the world. Reports praising him as 'The English Titian', 'the Painter of Eternal Truths' or 'England's Michelangelo' are an indication of the esteem in which he was held at the time.(15) Mary Watts survived the husband she revered as a genius by more than thirty years, during which time she saw tastes in art change completely with Watts's heroic Victorian paintings relegated to the basement of art galleries and museums whilst the Impressionists and Post-Impressionists gained in popularity and respect. Coincidentally, it was another Guildford resident, Roger Fry, who was instrumental in promoting this change of taste in England.

THE BLOOMSBURY SET AND GUILDFORD

By 1909 when artist and critic Roger Fry (1866-1934) designed his house, Durbins, overlooking the River Wey in Guildford, not only was the taste for heroic painting diminishing but the Arts and Crafts Movement itself was also losing its patronage. The preference for Classical architecture was re-asserting itself, but little could yet be heard of the revolutionary modern architectural ideas that were already emerging on the continent. Fry was the acknowledged leader of the English artistic Avant-Garde of 1910 and helped to introduce modern art into England, including the works of Cezanne, Matisse and Picasso. Whilst building his house Fry was also planning his second Post Impressionist Exhibition of 1911 which sent ripples, both positive and negative, through the London Art World. However, his radical ideas about art did not extend as far as architecture, as his house, although unique, appears rooted in Classical design.

Fry, a gifted amateur architect, took advantage of his sloping site by placing the entrance at the rear, or top of the slope, to allow him to make use of split-level planning. Upon entering the house the main double height living room is approached down a half flight of steps, whilst half a flight up is his studio, dining room and gallery. Bedrooms are all at second floor level under the mansard roof. The plan of the house is symmetrical, as is the garden elevation with its eighteenth century French flavour. The only link the house has in common with the Arts and Crafts design is the use of natural materials and simple uncluttered spaces. Fry consulted Gertrude Jekyll about the garden which was laid out in five terraces creating an idyllic spot for Fry's two children to spend their childhood, reared by his sister during his wife's long illness. *(See Fig. XVI Colour illustration: Durbins 1910 by renowned art critic Roger Fry)*

Durbins became a suburban retreat for Fry's avant-garde colleagues and he was visited by Clive and Vanessa Bell, contemporary painter Duncan Grant and various well known writers including E.M. Forster, Leonard and Virginia Wolff and John Masefield. Fry collaborated with his friends Duncan Grant and Vanessa Bell in painting a large fresco inspired by Matisse's 'Dancers', which is still in the entrance hall of the house; each painter was responsible for one semi-abstract nude in a primary colour, Grant's in red, Bell's in yellow and Fry's in blue. In spirit and style this amateur but playful mural was of completely different character to the academic allegorical paintings preserved in the Watts Gallery only a few miles distant, and it represented the advent of a new era.

GARDEN CITIES & SOCIAL HOUSING

The First World War was the death knell to Arts and Crafts architecture and design. In fact, the movement had been declining for a decade before that. In addition to changing moods and tastes, its patrons were finding real incomes dropping. The Liberal Government of 1906 with its policy of social reform levied severe tax rises, including Death Duties, a Super-Tax and Land Value duties, all of which reduced disposable income. The former patrons of the the Arts and Crafts found little to attract them in the avant garde of Fry, although their social ideals found expression in the Garden City Movement, and later in the 'New Town' movement which sought to provide a healthy and wholesome lifestyle for ordinary people away from the industrial slums of the cities. New planned developments with plenty of light and green space, schools, churches and recreation centres were to be built to provide dignified and spiritually fulfilled lives for their inhabitants, in a manner that referred back to the teachings of Morris and Ruskin. Ebenezer Howard's proposals for garden cities, published in 1898 in his book "A Peaceful Path to Real Reform", were expanded in his 1902 publication "Garden Cities of Tomorrow", when he proposed a ring of such developments around each metropolis, connected to both the capital and each other by high speed railways. Enlightened philanthropic employers like George Cadbury and Joseph Rowntree were already building model villages for their workers following on from the famous example of Sir Titus Salts' village of Saltaire near Bradford, but the new Garden City Movement was not tied to a single employer. The architectural practice of Parker and Unwin was at the forefront of the movement, being responsible for Letchworth Garden City of 1903 in Hertfordshire and Hampstead Garden Suburb of 1912.

Guildford had its own early pioneers in this provision of improved housing for the working classes. In 1862, an entrepreneurial doctor, Thomas Sells, commissioned Henry Peak to lay out an ambitious estate almost as large in area as the existing town. Charlotteville, as it was known, was a mixed development of artisan cottages and comfortable detached villas, complete with shops, pubs and, later, a large school.

Other experiments included "Caxton Gardens", a development of 34 houses built in 1907 by the printing firm for worker tenants who would own their own homes after 20 years rental. In 1915, Dennis Brothers and the Council combined to provide much needed housing at Dennisville, on land owned by the Council. After World War I, pressure for housing was intense and, in 1919, The Onslow Village Association was formed, based on Ebenezer Howard's Garden City concept. Mr Litchfield, a prime mover in the Association had been involved at Hampstead Garden Suburb and the aim was to provide decent, low rent homes that would eventually become the property of the occupiers. A self-contained community was to be established with its own shops, schools and factories all to be built in pleasant, landscaped surroundings. The project generated great good-will with Lord Onslow of Clandon selling 646 acres of land to the Association at one quarter of its commercial value, whilst the Borough Council loaned money at very competitive rates and both Lord Onslow and a local resident, Herbert Powell, generously invested personal funds (16). Onslow Village eventually grew to 450 dwellings all built in an informal vernacular style which emanated from the Arts and Crafts movement. Clay tiled roofs, walls of local bricks, leaded casement windows and generously sized private gardens are all features of the original houses in the village, now a conservation area.

A POSTSCRIPT

The aesthetic ideals of the Arts and Crafts Movement, although watered down, were never forsaken by many ordinary people and the vast numbers of detached and semi-detached houses which sprung up along commuter lines more often than not harked back to an old England of country cottages with hand crafted front doors, picturesque porches, tile hanging and half-timbering, surrounded by well tended cottage gardens. The peculiar affinity between the English and their idealized countryside with its picturesque buildings remains as strong today as it did in the late nineteenth century.

NOTES

(1) Chamberlin, Russel "Guildford, A Biography", Macmillan 1970, p.14.

(2) The Queen Anne style was based on Classical substantial middle rank houses of the late seventeenth and early eighteenth century. The English Baroque (Fr. bizarre, fantastic or irregular) style of the late sixteenth and early seventeenth centuries is based on flamboyant late Renaissance architecture, as represented by Bernini in Italy and Sir John Vanbrugh (Blenheim Palace) and Nicholas Hawksmoor in England.

(3) This exchange appears in "Norman Shaw" by Andrew Saint, p.311.

(4) "Surrey Advertiser', 18 November 1905, p.3.

(5) A model of the lodge featured in the Lutyens exhibition at the Hayward Gallery and is now on loan from the Bray Estate to the Shere Museum.

(6) Jekyll, Gertrude, "House and Garden"

(7) Quotation from Peter Davey's "Arts .and Crafts Architecture-The Search for Earthly Paradise", p.82.

(8) The 1913 additions to the Sturgis House were designed by Herbert Baker whose work, mainly classical, includes the Secretariat in New Delhi and South Africa House in Trafalgar Square.

(9) This information is from the unpublished 'A' Level thesis by Cherry Gay, 1986, Priors Field School.

(10) Davey, Peter, "Arts and Crafts Architecture-The Search for Earthly Paradise", p. 95

(11) Quotation from Dr. George Williamson's "Guildford Charities - A Description of the Various Charities" Appertaining to the Town and Neighbourhood, Corporation of Guildford, 1931, pp 111-113.

(12) Pevsner, Nikolaus and Nairn, Ian, "The Buildings of England - Surrey", Penguin, 1990, p.72.

(13) A fuller description of the formation of The Old Guildford Society can be read in Russell Chamberlin's book, "Guildford-Town Under Siege", published to commemorate the Guildford Society's 50th Anniversary, 1987, pp.7-8.

(14) Peter Davey's "Arts and Crafts Architecture-The Search for Earthly Paradise", p. 167.

(15) Blunt, Wilfrid, "England's Michelangelo, A Biography of George Frederic Watts", Columbus Books, 1989.

(16) R. E. Chamberlin's chapter 'Shaping the Town' in his book "Guildford-A Biography" describes housing initiatives in Guildford.

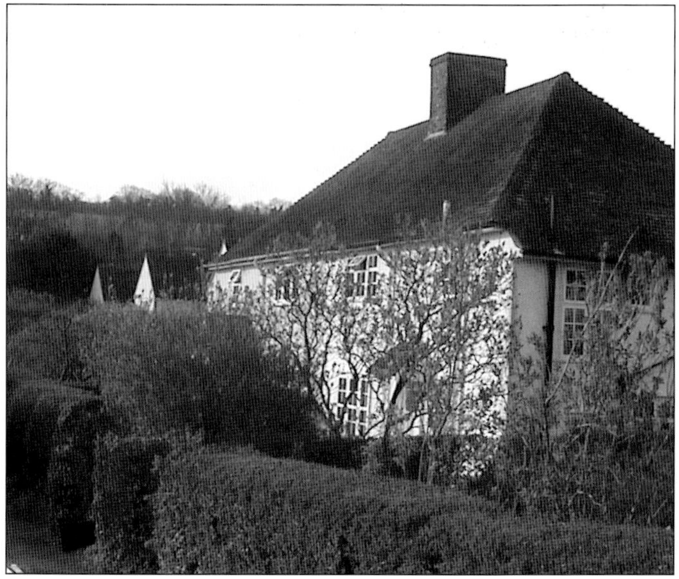

Fig. 34 View of Onslow Village today.

THE PLATES

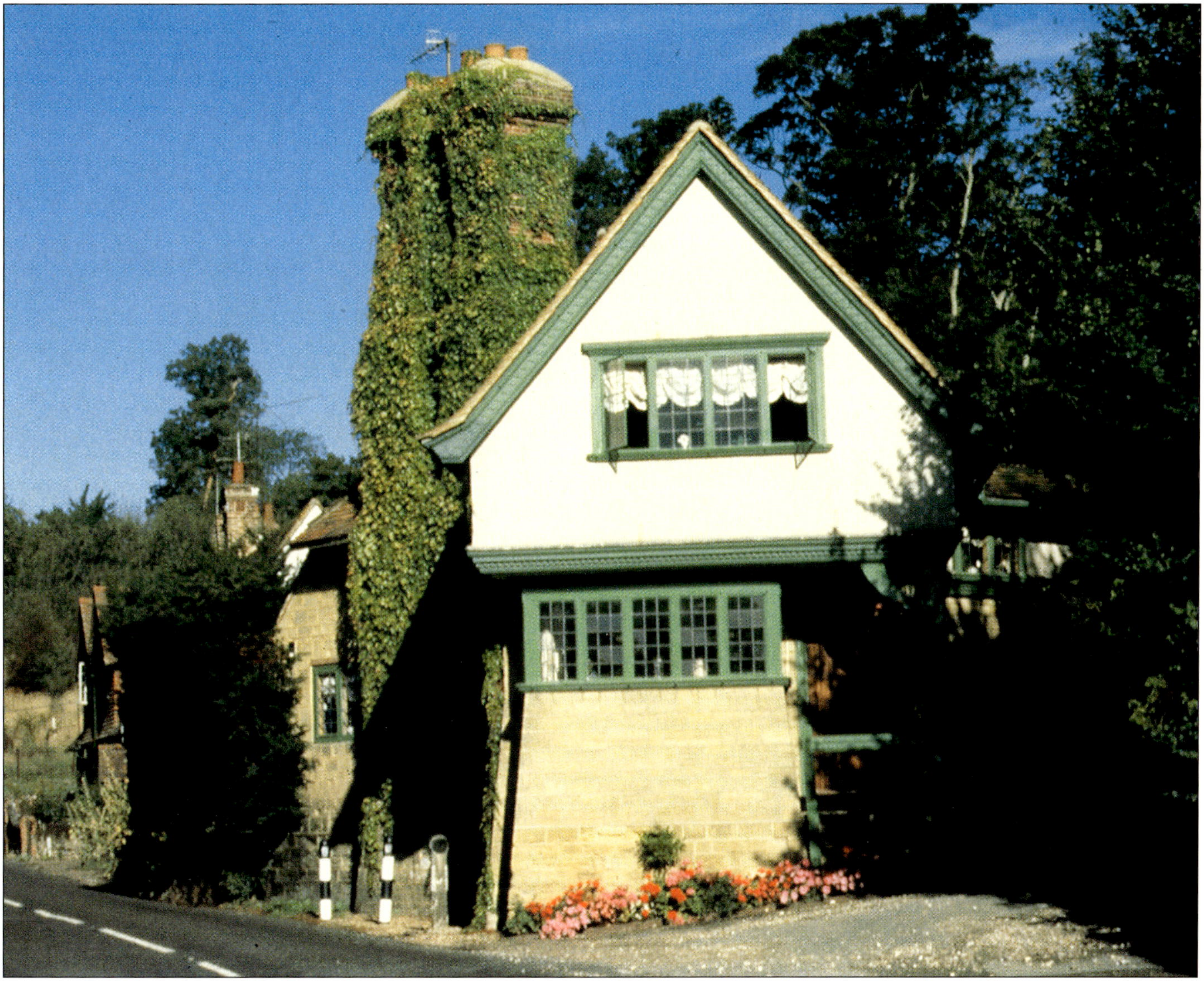

Fig. I: The Lodge (1894) in Shere by Edwin Lutyens.

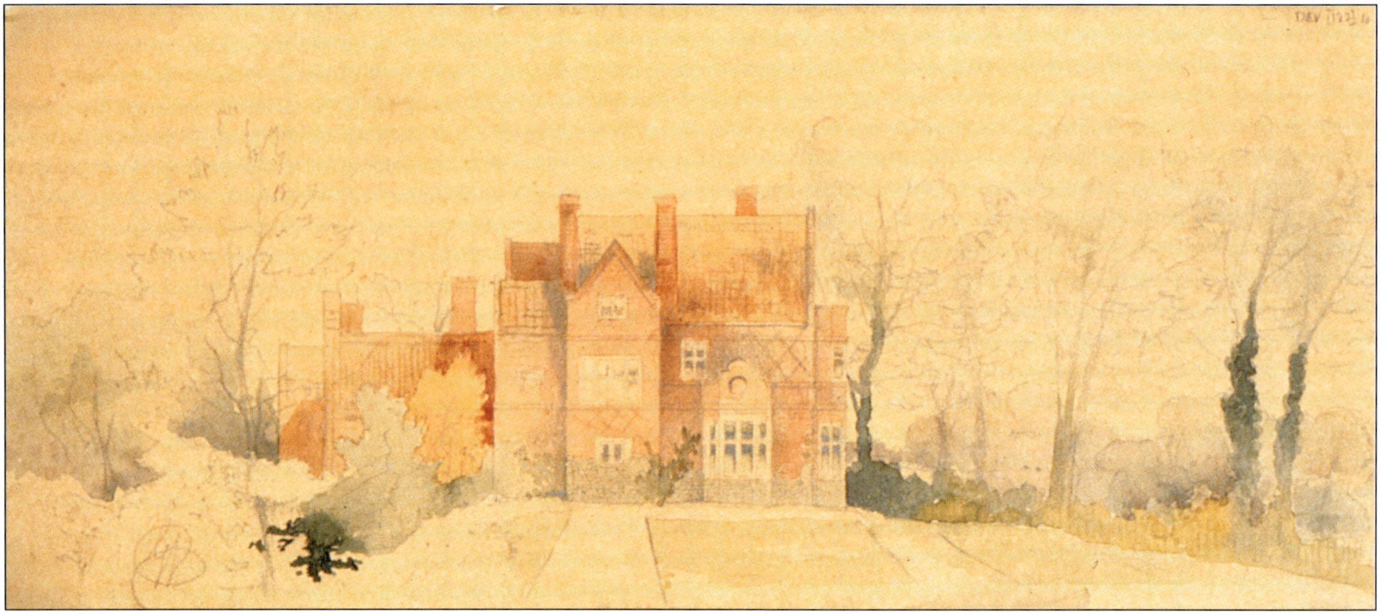

Fig. II *Watercolour of Send Holme by the Architect George Devey. Side elevation of Send Holme* (1871). Courtesy of the British Architectural Library, RIBA

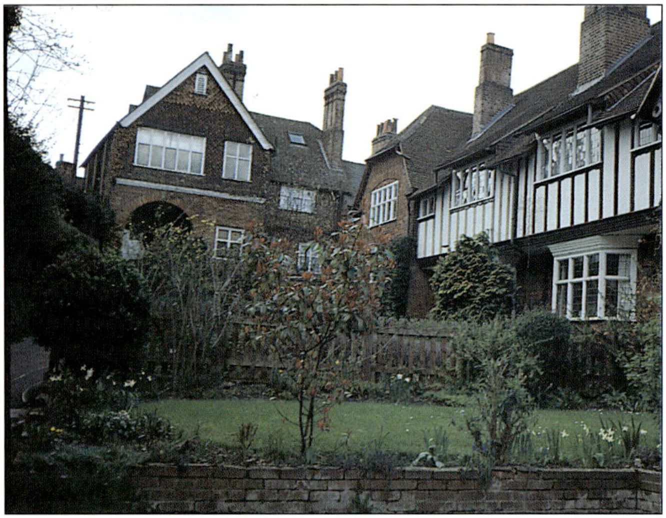

Fig. III *The Valley* (1881), *an 'Old English" group of semi-detached houses in St. Catherine's, designed in the style of Norman Shaw*

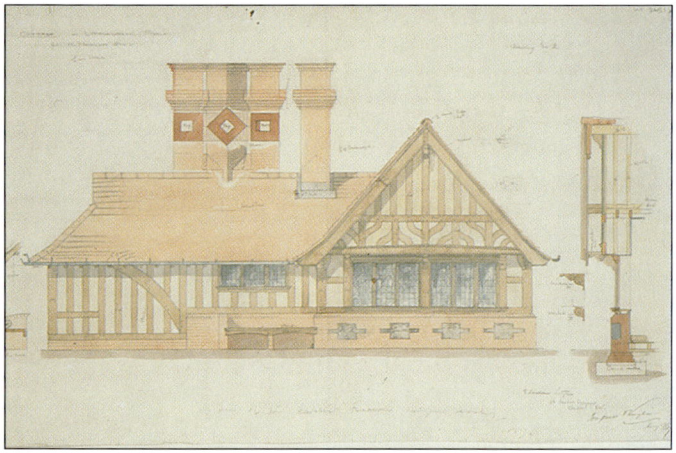

Fig. IV *Lutyens' design for a cottage at Littleworth Cross, near Guildford* (1889) *which was never built.* Courtesy of the British Architectural Library, RIBA. *The drawing shows the architect's appreciation of traditional timber detailing , note the study of the rafter feet.*

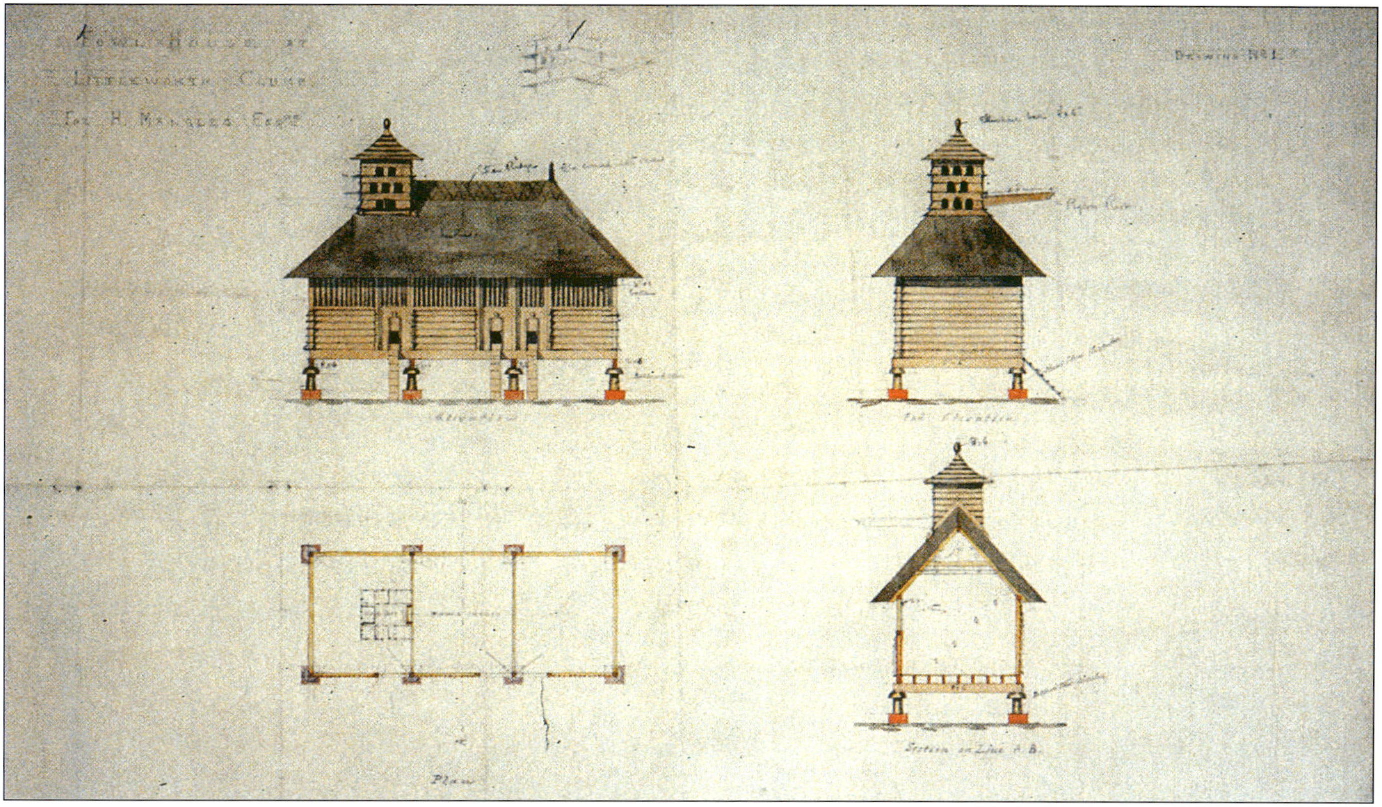

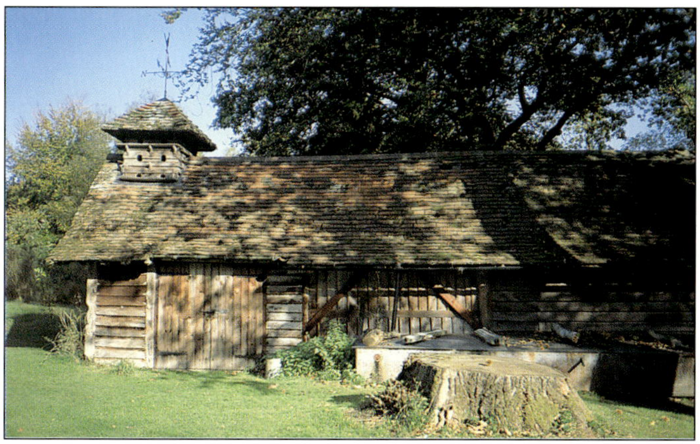

Above: Fig. V Lutyens' drawing of the Fowl House (1889)
Courtesy of the Birish Architectural Library, RIBA.

Left: Fig. VI Lutyens' Fowl House as built at Littleworth Cross.

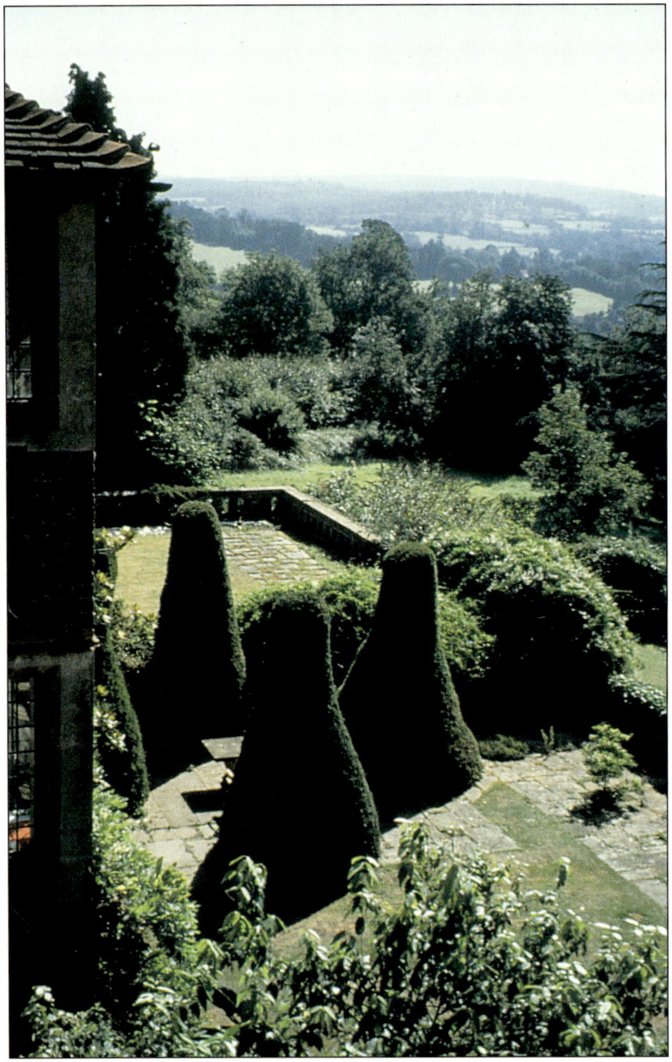

Above: Fig. VII View from Chinthurst Hill. A Lutyens' house in a Jekyll garden (1894)

Right: *Fig. VIII Presentation drawings by C F A Voysey of entrance and garden elevations of Norney Grange* (1897).
Courtesy of British Architectural Library, RIBA.

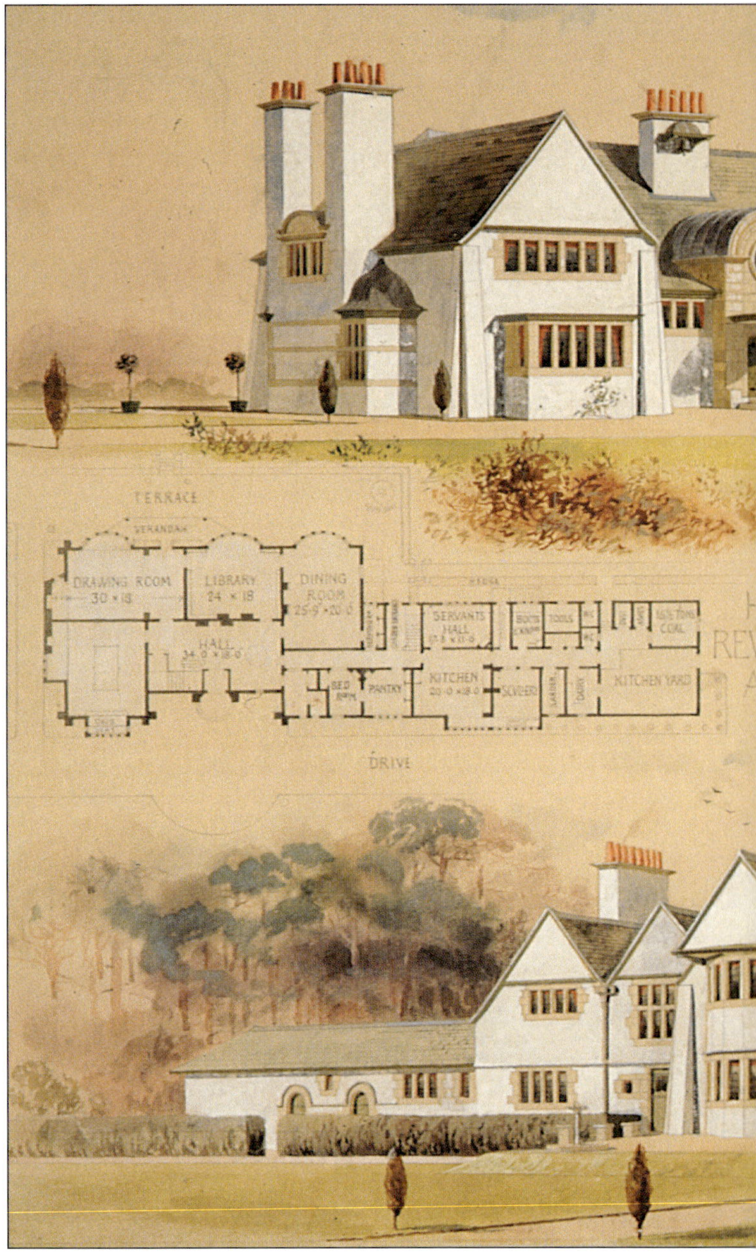

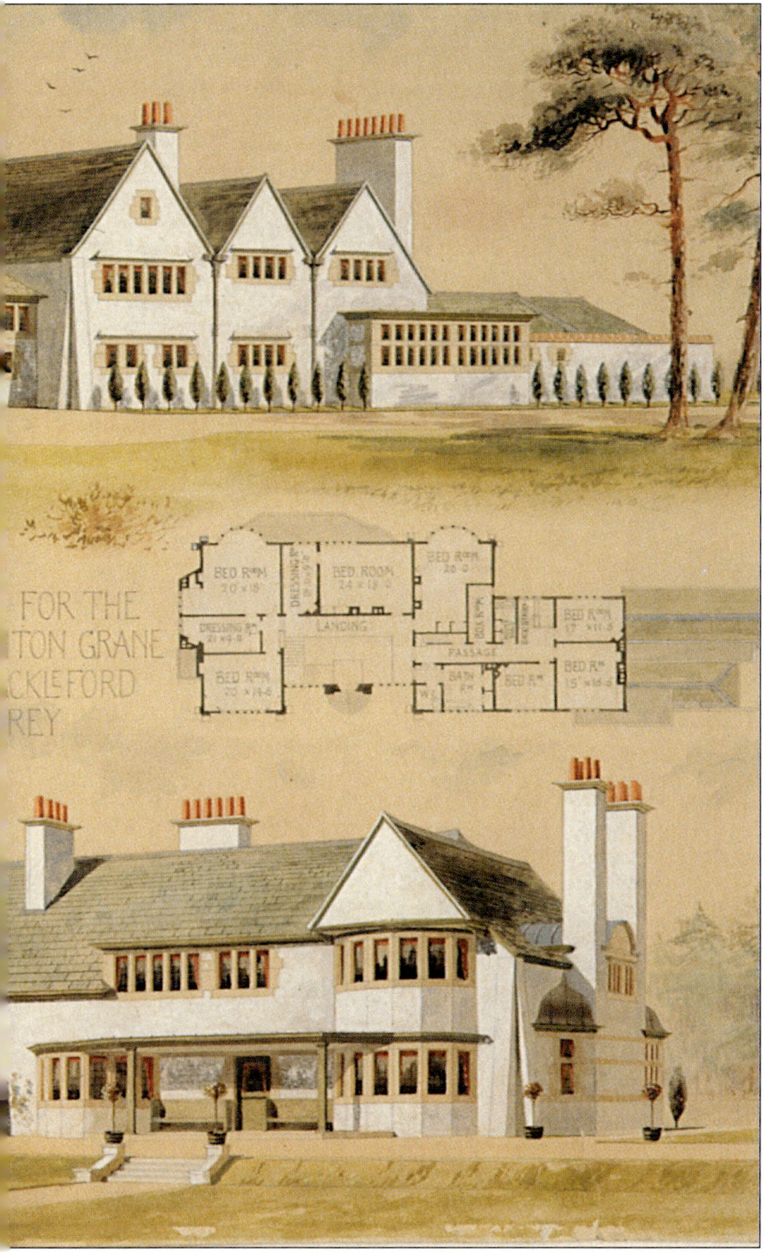

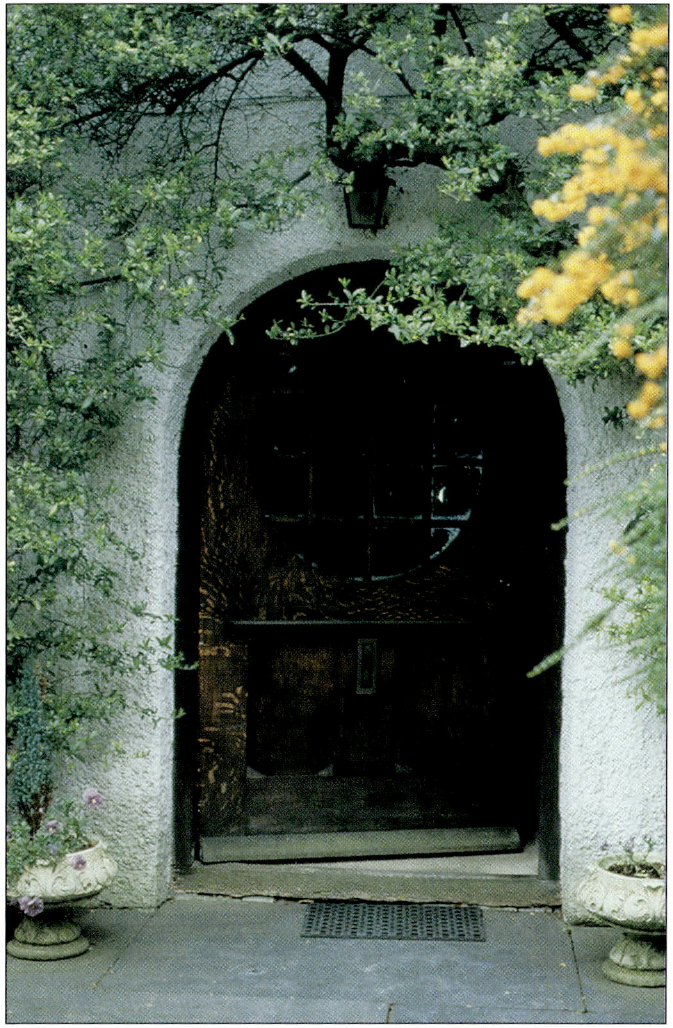

Fig. IX *Wide, round headed oak door at Littleholme, by Voysey. A typical Arts and Crafts feature.*

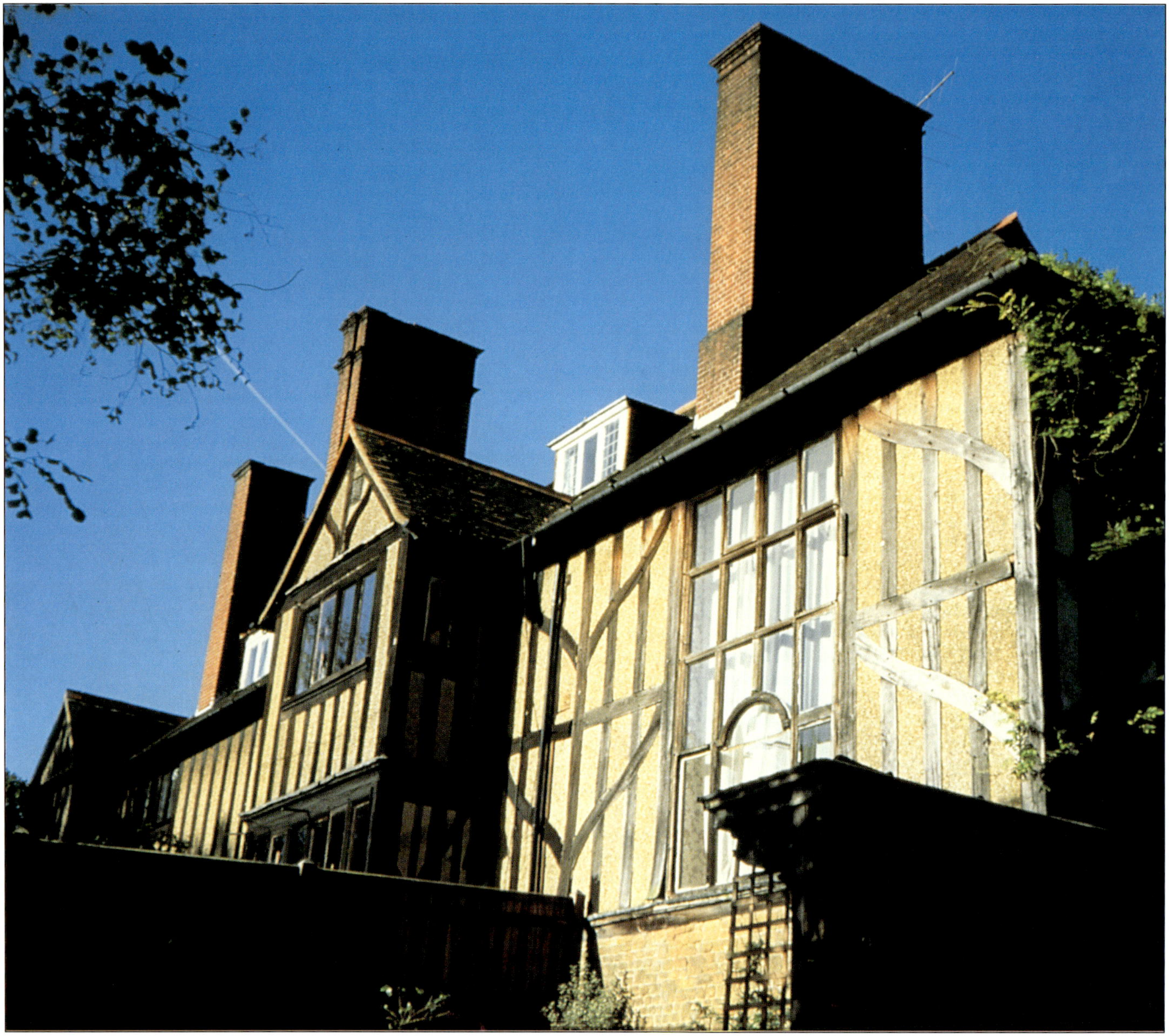

Fig. X Limnerslease, Compton. Designed by Sir Ernest George for the painter G.F. Watts in 1891.

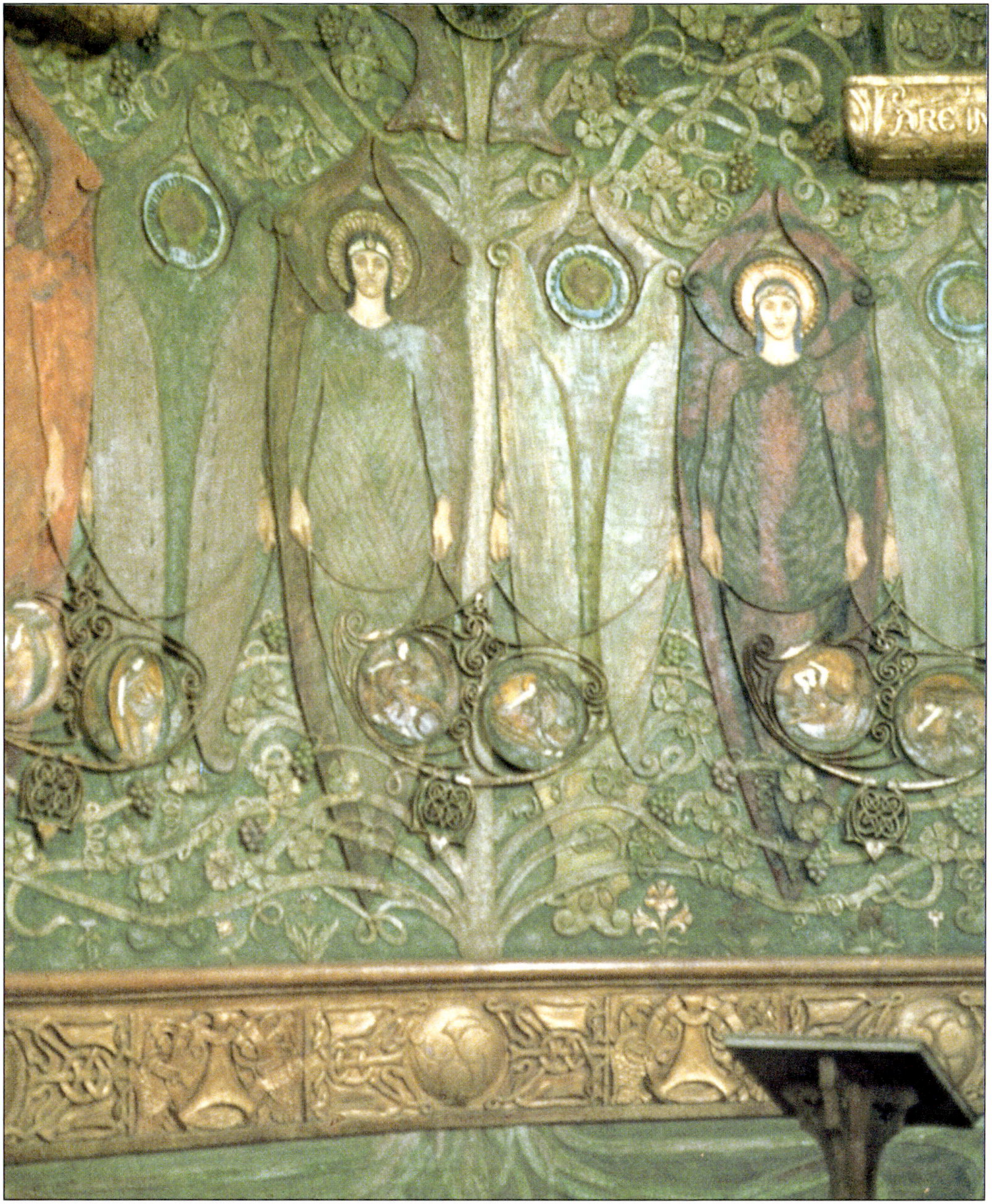

Fig. XI *Watts Chapel interior gesso decoration depicting the Tree of Life, by Mary Watts and villagers.* c 1901. Courtesy of the Watts Gallery.

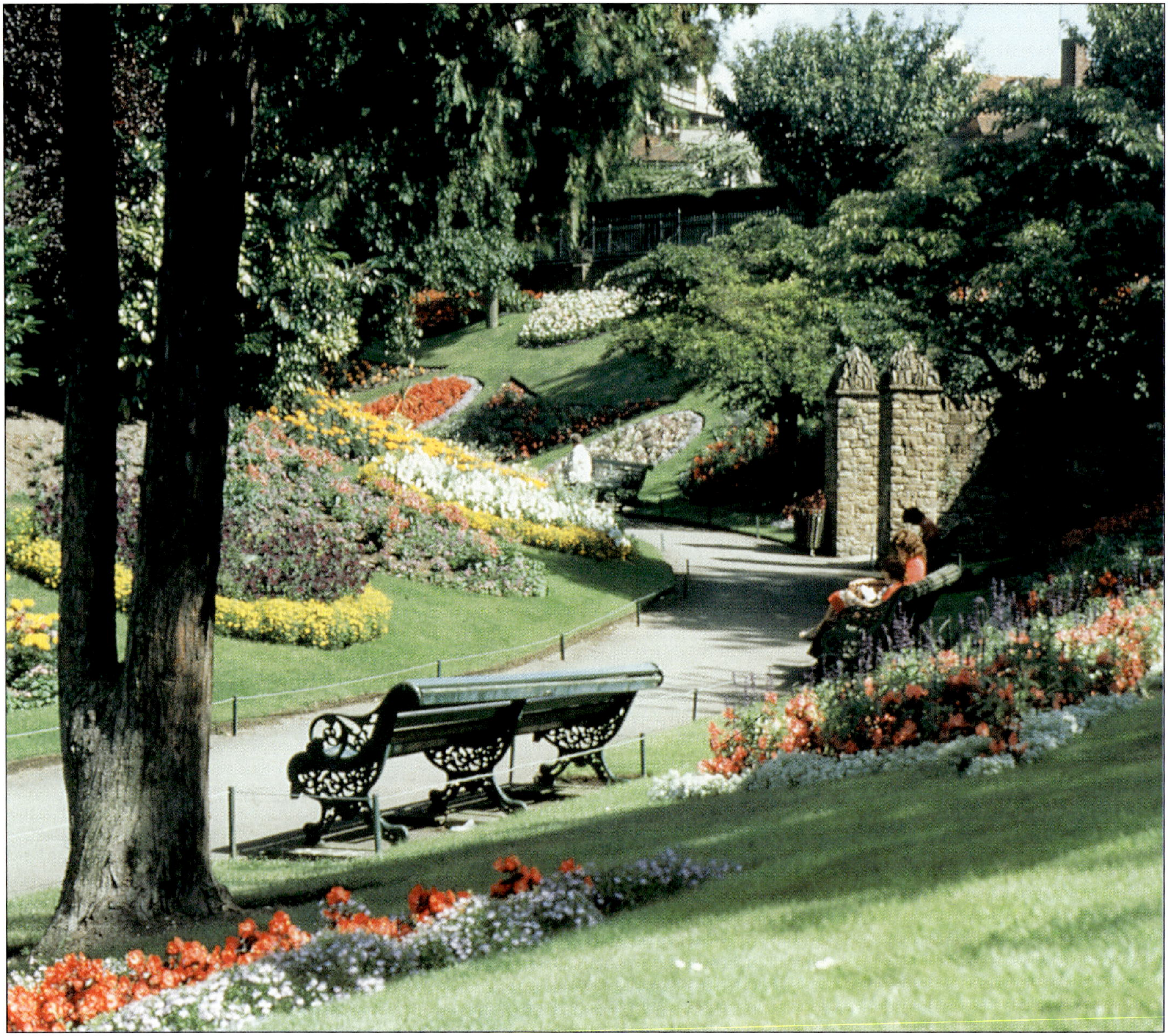

Fig. XII Example of formal bedding system at the Castle Grounds, Guildford. Courtesy of Guildford Borough Council.

Fig. XIII Gravetye Manor, *West* Sussex. *An* example of informal planting.

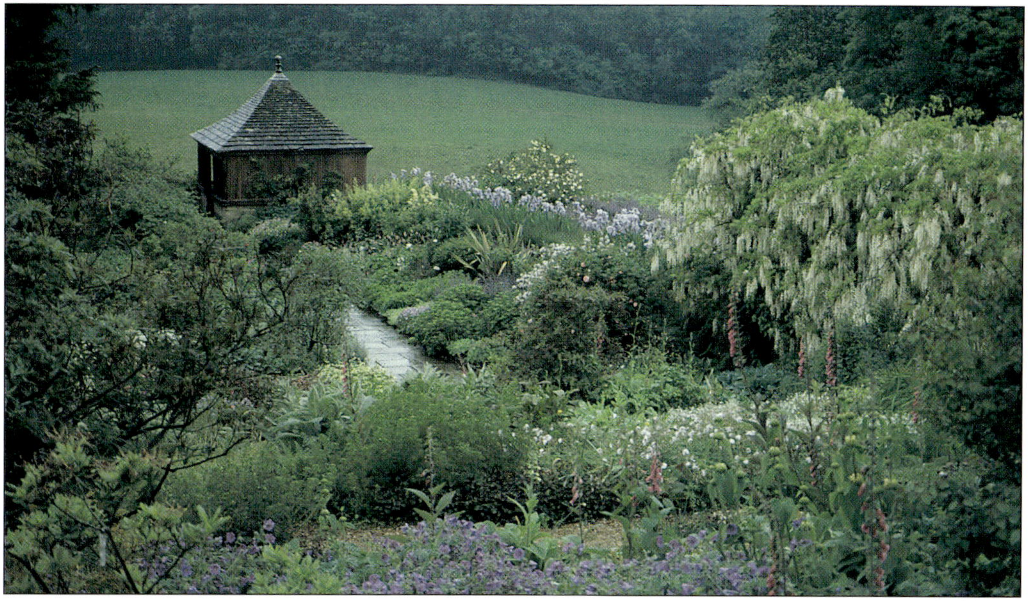

Fig. XIV The South Garden at Hatchlands which has recently been restored by the National Trust to Gertrude Jekyll's original design

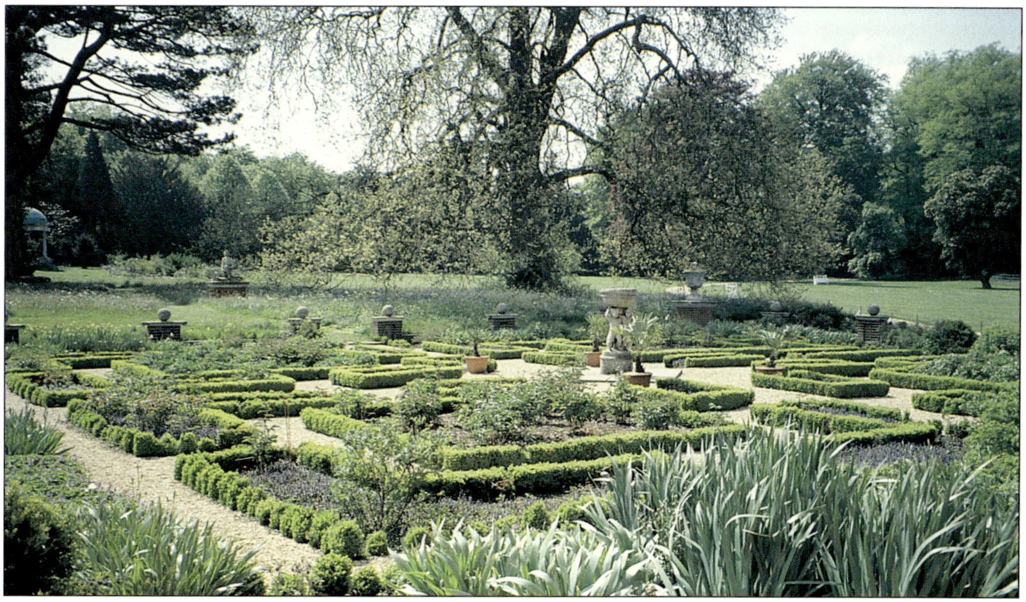

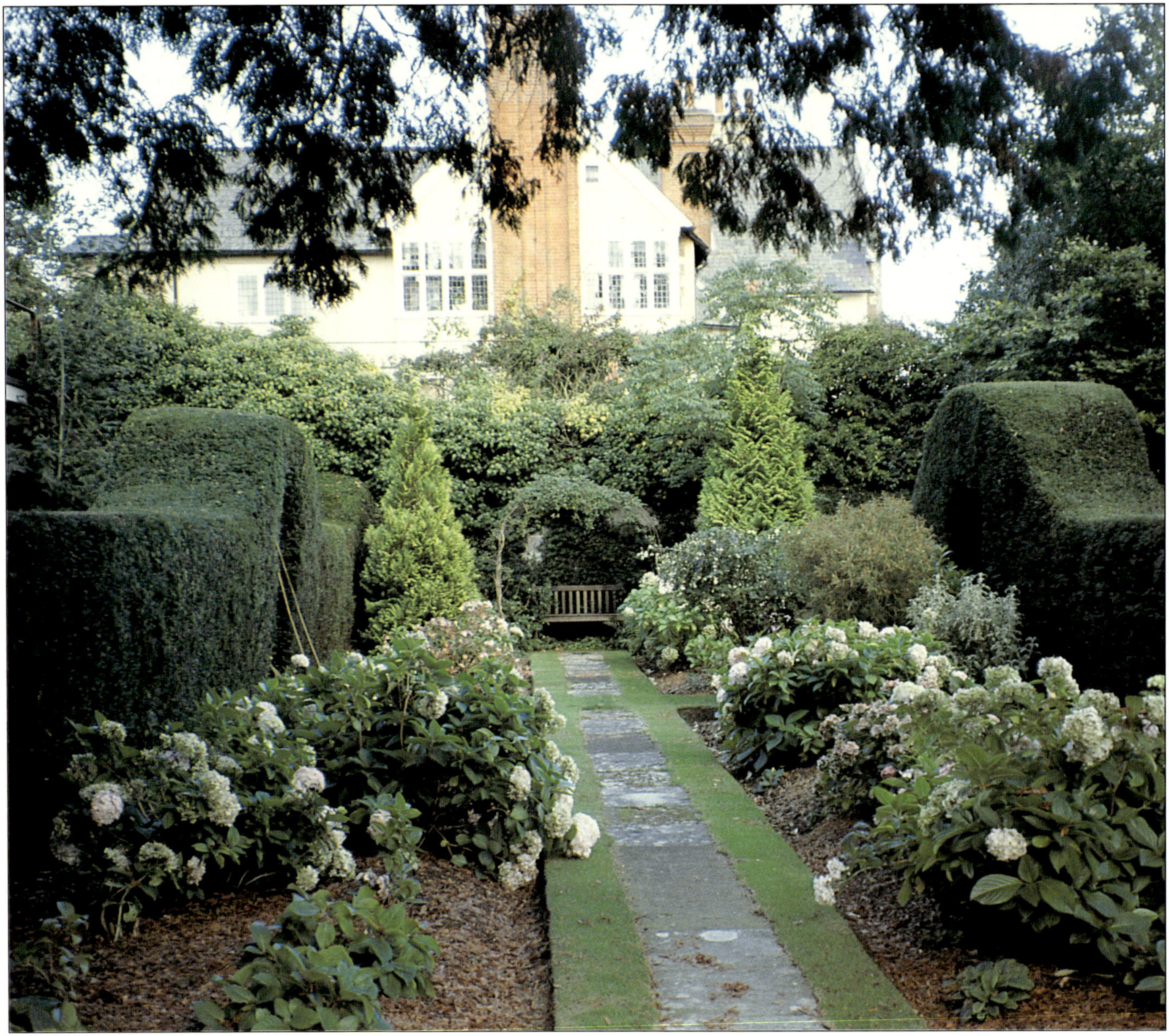

Fig. XV Piccards Rough Garden, Yew hedges framing the original vista, now obscured by subdivision.

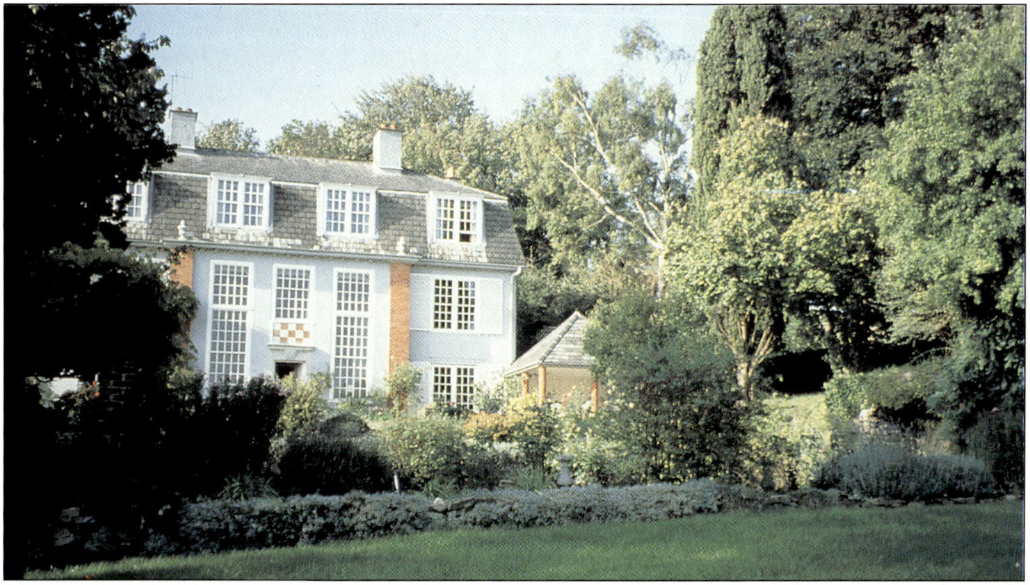

Left: Fig. XVI. Durbins, house designed by Roger Fry for himself in 1910.Original garden was by Gertrude Jekyll, some features remain.

Below: Fig. XVII Compton Pottery Seats in the Japanese Garden at Piccards Rough.

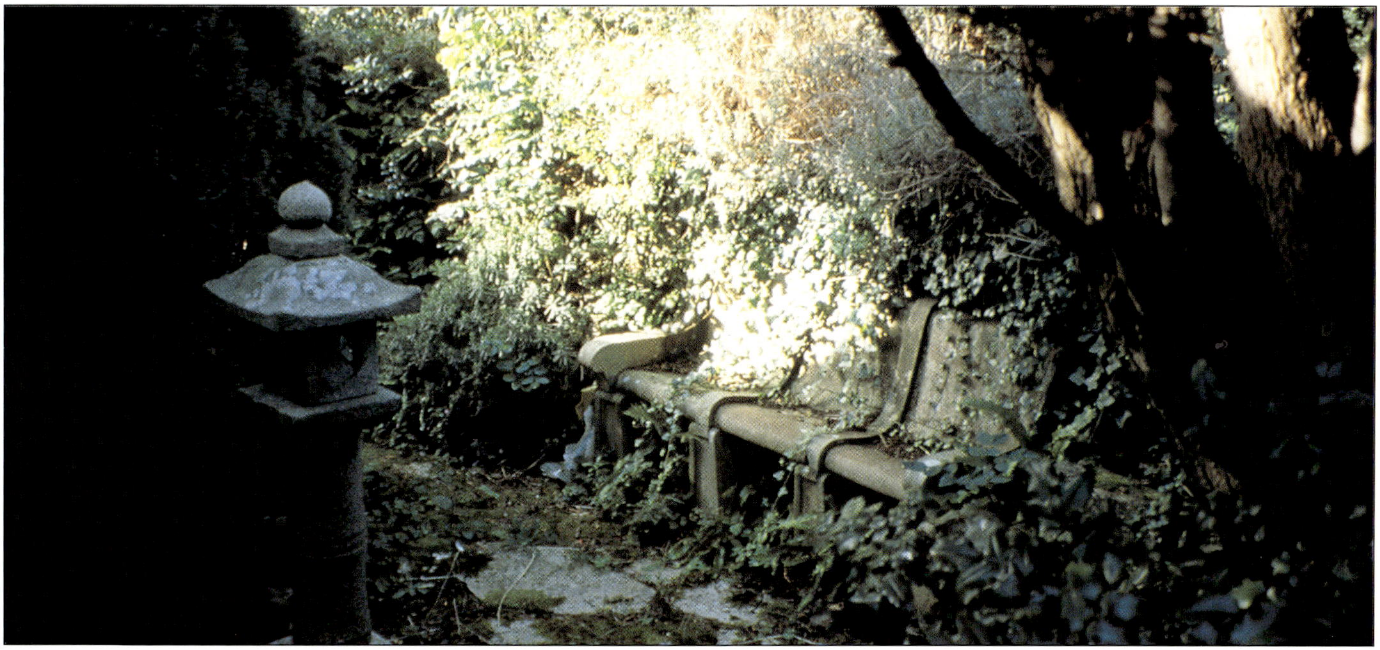

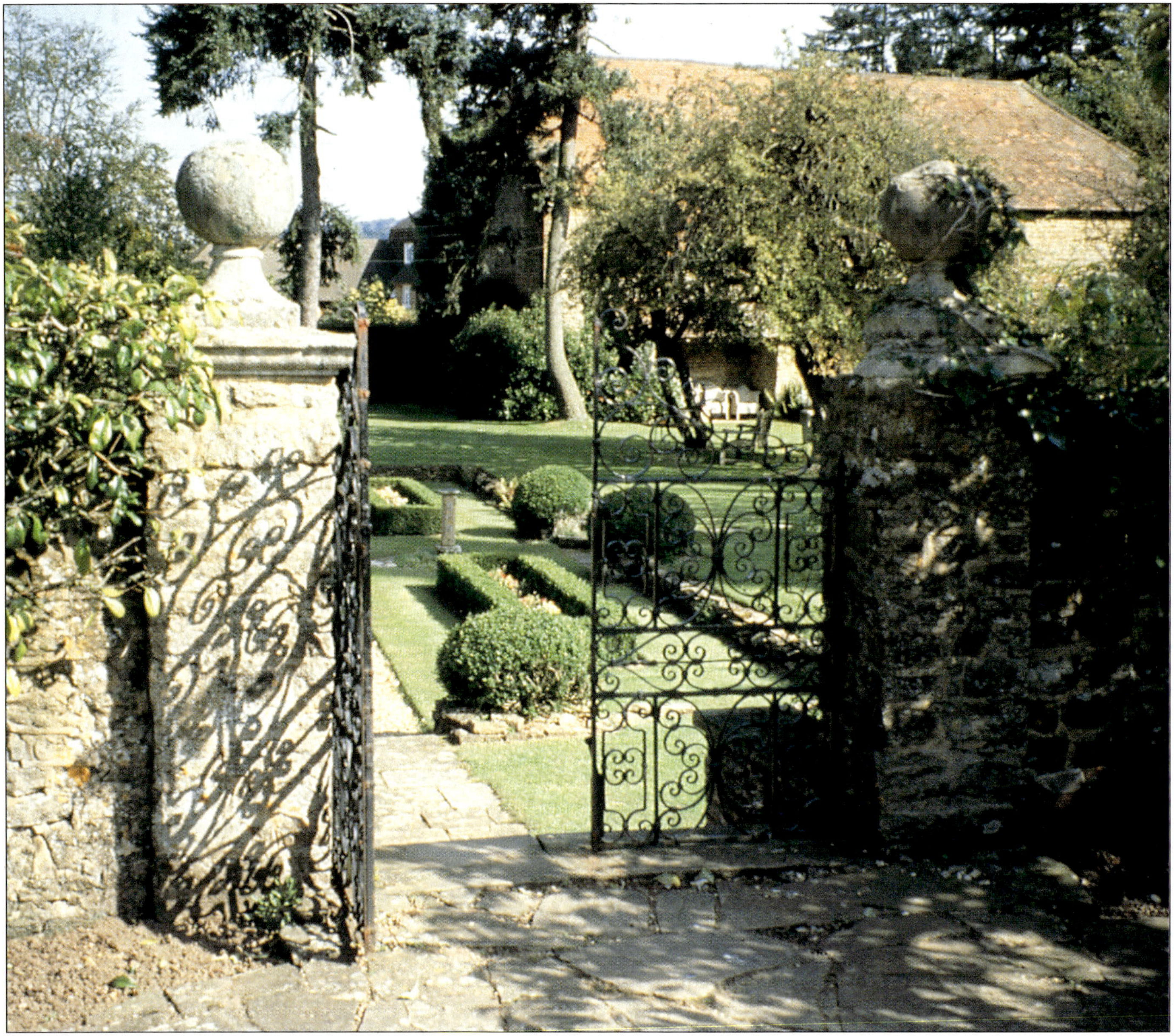

Fig. XVIII Piccards Manor: *An example of an Arts and Crafts style garden added to complement an existing sixteenth century farmhouse.*

ARTS AND CRAFTS GARDENS IN AND AROUND GUILDFORD

GARDENS

The Arts and Crafts garden, with its roots in the cottage gardens of generations of country folk and illustrated in the delicate watercolours of painters such as Helen Allingham, seems so well known to us today that it is difficult to believe that such gardens were not always fashionable.

The movement to conserve and protect our heritage of plants and the concept of growing plants in areas where they suit the landscape, i.e. taking account of the soil, climate and topography, are so ingrained in our present gardening culture that to appreciate its development we must step back and review the gardens of Victorian England.

Then, geometric gardens were the vogue – with gravel parterres, box scroll designs, box parterres and dwarf plants for bedding. As a contrast to this emphasis on the horizontal, standard plants were used to give a vertical dimension. Exotic plants were much prized and frequently used – one such, the Monkey Puzzle tree, is still to be seen in suburban gardens.

The bedding system was the most popular style of gardening at this time. Plants were grown in thin lines of colour, with the occasional use of 'dot' plants for contrast. Today, this system survives mainly in municipal gardens, especially at tourist centres, where summer visitors admire the juxtaposition of many bright colours and involved patterns. *(See Fig. XII Colour illustration. Example of formal bedding system at the Castle Grounds, Guildford.)*

Inevitably, there was a reaction to the bedding system, championed initially by William Robinson, author of "The English Flower Garden", first published in 1883. His own garden at Gravetye Manor, near East Grinstead, West Sussex, can be visited as the house is now a hotel. *(See Fig. XIII Colour illustration. Gravetye Manor, West Sussex. An example of naturalistic planting.)*

Another strand in the formation of the Arts and Crafts garden was that in the 1860's there was a revival of interest in rustic work – pergolas, arbours, bridges and trellis-work made from unbarked wood, a precursor to the interest in old building techniques favoured by Arts and Crafts designers.

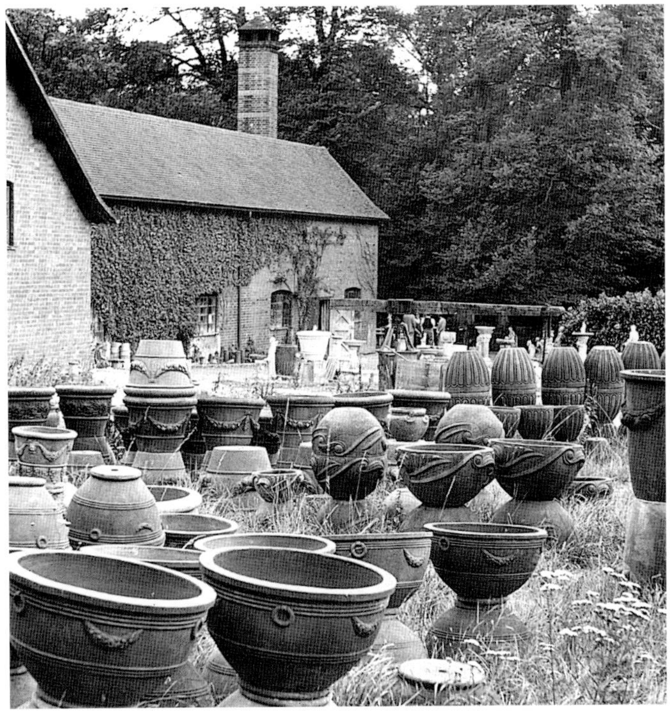

Fig. 35 Terracota pots at Compton Pottery

THE ARTS AND CRAFTS GARDEN

It is not possible to define as a particular style the Arts and Crafts garden. They came in all shapes, depending upon the location, topography, local building materials and the design of the house of which the garden was an integral feature. However, it is possible to pick out various features which were frequently associated with the Arts and Crafts garden:

1. **Local building materials** were used in the construction of the garden – for paving, steps, dry stone walls and pergolas (either constructed of local stone, bricks or tiles, with oak beams, or completely of timber).

2. **Plants and trees** were indigenous (native), or at least suited to the site, as opposed to the trend for introducing exotics newly arrived from abroad, harking back to the cottage garden tradition of herbs, roses and herbaceous flowers.

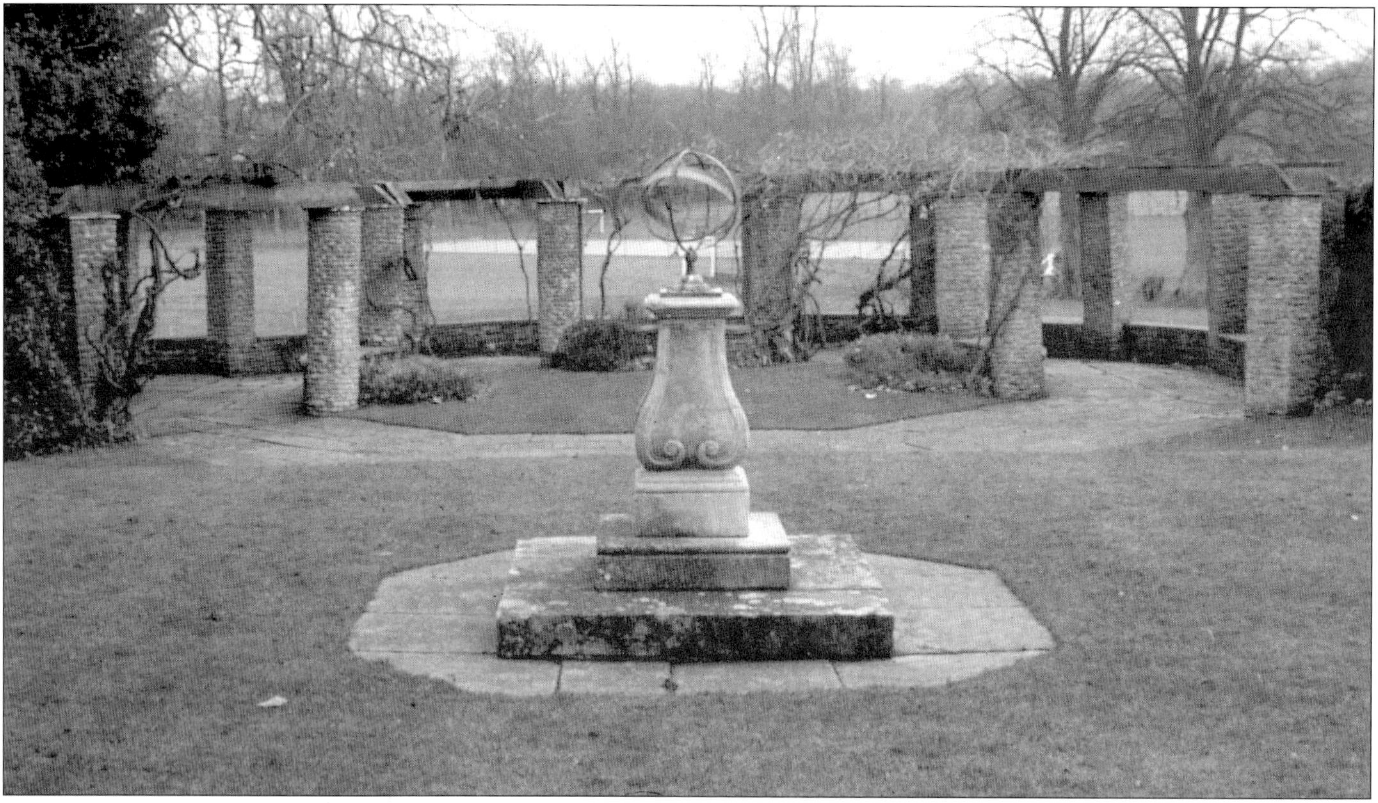

Fig. 36 Recently restored pergola at Aldro School, Shackleford (formerly Hall Place), part of a Jekyll garden design, constructed of local Bargate Stone, and timber salvaged from the school grounds after the 1987 hurricane.

3. Garden features: pergolas originated in Italy as a support for vines, designers began to use them as a method of extending the house into the garden, usually planted with Wisteria or Laburnum inside, and Roses and Clematis outside; pools, tanks, formal ponds – especially a dipping pool for filling watering cans on dry sandy soil, were a useful as well as an attractive element in the garden; seats, walls and gateways and summer-houses or gazebos.

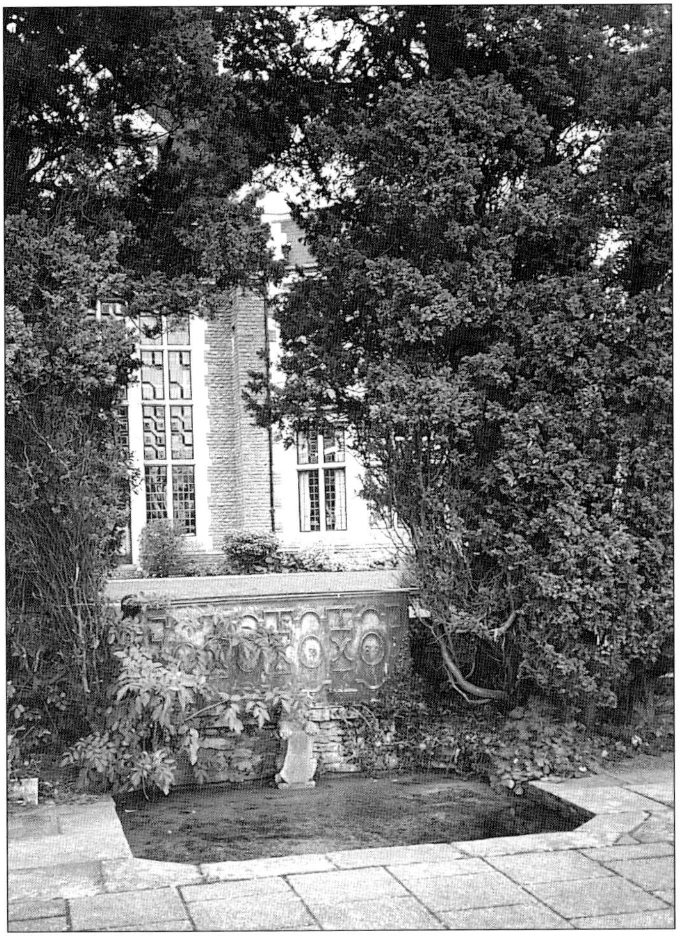

Fig. 37 *Water tank and pool at Aldro School Shackleford.*

4. Hedges and topiary: Hedges, usually formal, and either low in Box, or high for enclosure in Yew, were frequent features in Arts and Crafts gardens. The hedges defined areas, provided backdrops to herbaceous borders and by their visual enclosure helped create the element of surprise as the visitor walked from one area to another. From the use of hedges evolved another element which became the trademark of the Arts and Crafts garden – topiary. The clipping of hedges into interesting shapes – such as birds, became very popular, though few examples survive in Guildford's Arts and Crafts gardens. (*See Fig. XV Colour illustration Piccards Rough Garden, Yew hedges framing the original vista, now obscured by subdivision*)

5. Statues and Sundials: Lead statues, terracotta sundials, bird tables and bowls were frequently used to enhance Arts and Crafts gardens, sometimes in conjunction with water features, or at the end of walks or views.

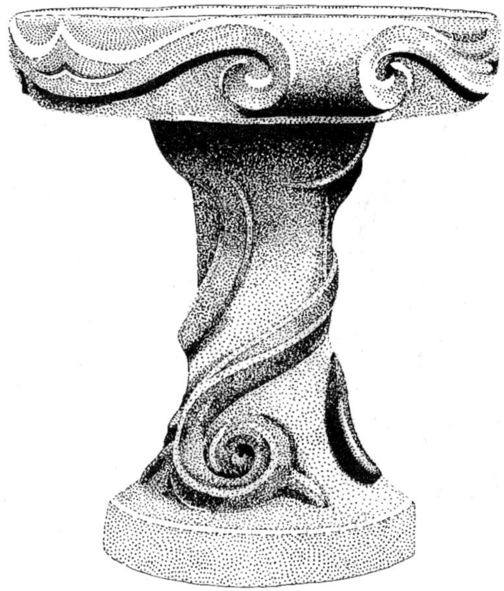

Fig. 38: *sketch of Scroll bird bath with Cobra pedastal, product of Compton Pottery*

THE COMPTON POTTERY AND GARDEN ORNAMENT

Ornaments for Arts and Crafts gardens could take many forms, from well-heads and wall fountains associated with water features, sundials and seats, planters and tubs, to statues and vases.

> *"Lead holds indisputably first place as the material for garden ornaments in England; but it is apt to be expensive, and cement, if rightly used and coloured, makes a satisfactory substitute. There remains terracotta, which can be admirable if of quiet colouring and attractive texture; but the shiny red of some clays is hard and unpleasant. Some delightful garden pottery of subdued reds and greys is made by the Potters' Arts Guild at Compton, Surrey, the enterprise of Mrs G F Watts. The bird bath, illustrated in another chapter, is a good example of the service ceramics can do to the garden, and there are many satisfactory bowls to be had in the same material, modelled on simple lines and sparingly decorated with swags of fruit and the like simple devices."* (1)

The work of the Potters' Arts Guild was a living example of Arts and Crafts ideals. The venture had its beginnings in the move to Compton in 1891 of the artist G F Watts, and his second wife, Mary, to their new home, Limnerslease (painters house).

In December 1900 Mary had written to a Mr James Nicol, asking if he would consider coming to Compton to manage a pottery run on commercial lines.

> *"I believe* (she wrote) *that neither man nor woman can do better than try to make a delightful village industry – beautiful things beautifully made, by people in beautiful country."* (2)

After he refused her offer, Mary wrote again to Mr Nicol, who then came to Compton, stayed, and the venture flourished, producing terracotta garden urns, sundials, ornaments, benches and church fonts to her designs. Orders came from all over England and the Commonwealth, with interesting pieces purchased for the garden of Pretoria's Parliament House and, closer to home, Art Nouveau tombstones for the Compton Chapel graveyard.

> *"The Potters Wheel...In a picturesque tiled "workshop" nestling on the side of that curious Surrey ridge, the Hog's Back, Mrs G F Watts has comfortably housed the work which has only in the last year been growing from the recreative evening class into a village industry, the first object of which is to establish a little colony, in the heart of the country, of intelligent happy workers, who, trained in eye, mind, and hand, will take pride in making, as the guild of artists did long ago in Italy, their village name known in association with their craft. The great question of decentralization from our large cities is, at the same time, always kept in view. The progress already made is astonishing, and the work in terracotta turned out here is quite as good as that coming from Italy. Vases and pots of exquisitely graceful outline, plain or ornamented with designs of interlacing serpents or linked bands, richly worked tiles and panels, some meant to be built up into great centrepots, others intended for decoration, garden seats, sundials ranging from simplicity to elaborateness – these are some of the things to be seen stacked in the showroom or lying about outside."* (3)

A 1913 Catalogue of "The Potters' Arts Guild, Mrs G F Watts' Village Industry, Compton, Guildford" (4) states on the cover:

"Designers and Manufacturers of
Artistic Garden Pots, Sundials, Birds' Baths, Birds' Feeding
Tables, etc, etc
In Red and Gray Terra Cotta

For particulars of Memorials, Statuettes, Glazed and
Coloured Wares, etc.
please apply to the Manager."

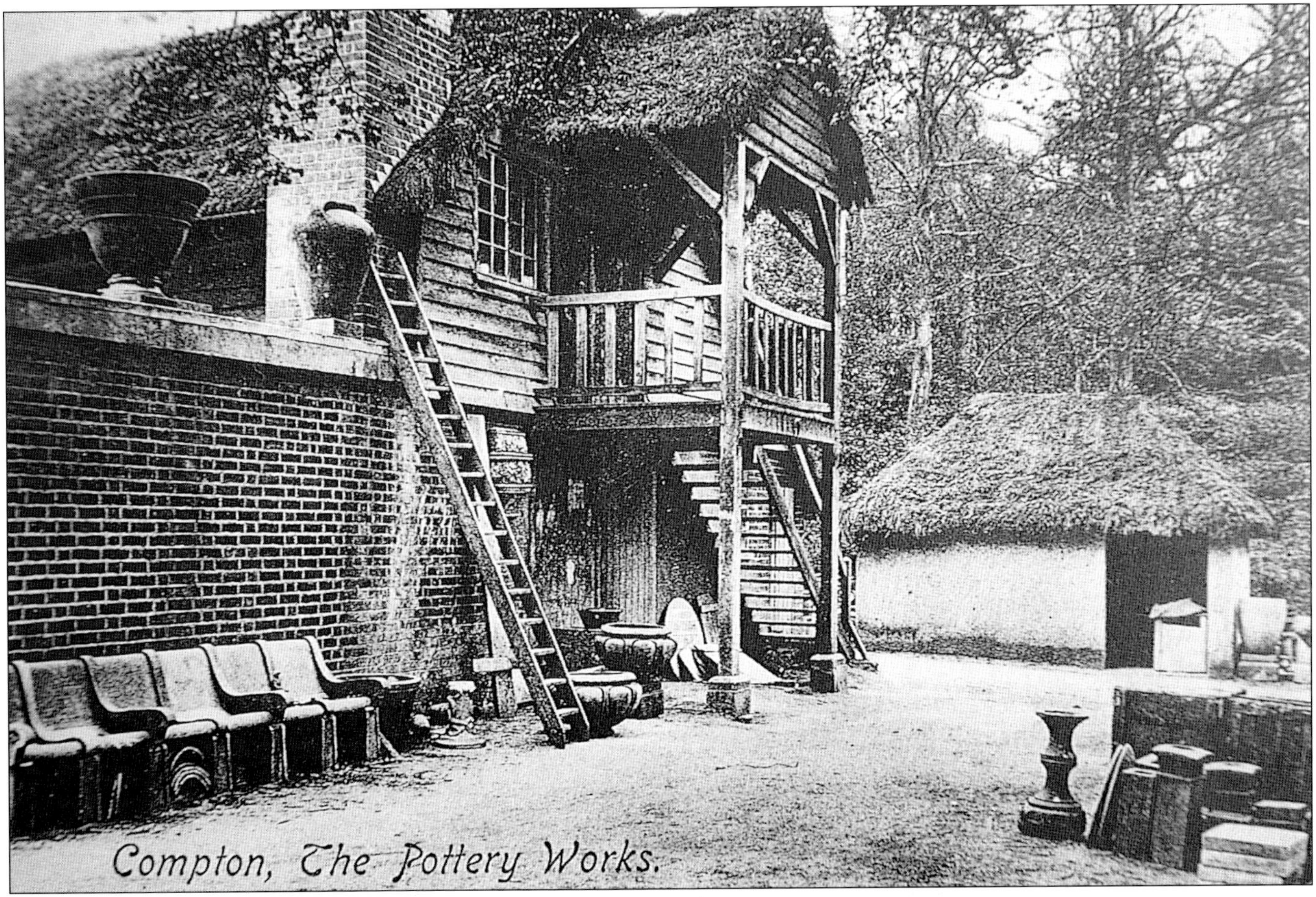

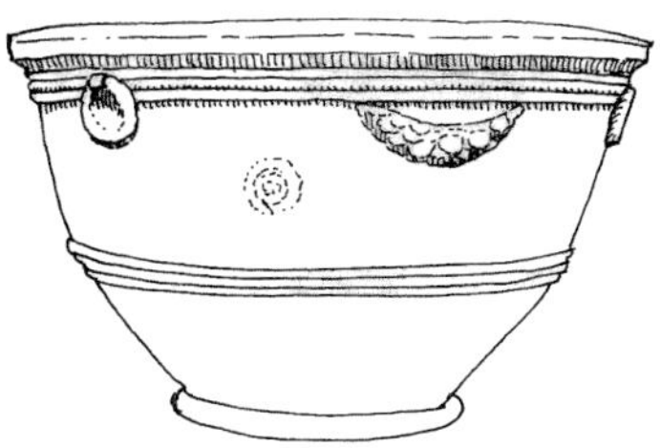

Left: Fig. 39a: Jekyll pot, product of Compton Pottery.

Above: Fig. 39b: Compton, The Pottery Works with examples of its products stored outside. Note the heather thatch on the buildings which has been replaced following a fire.

GERTRUDE JEKYLL

Many Arts and Crafts architects were competent amateur gardeners, but all acknowledged the debt they owed to one woman, from whom they learned so much about garden design, plants and trees, and the use of colour in planting schemes – her name was Gertrude Jekyll.

Gertrude Jekyll was born in London on 19 November 1843, one of six children, to comfortably well off and artistically aware parents. In 1848, the family moved to Bramley House, three miles south-west of Guildford. In the idyllic surroundings of a rambling country house, the young Gertrude received not only the benefits of a good education, but also had the freedom to explore the immediate environs of the park and later the surrounding Surrey countryside.

With her dog for company and mounted on her pony, she explored the nearby villages, learning to love not only the way of life of country people but also the skills of the various craftsmen. This appreciation of traditional skills and crafts was often mentioned years later in her books, and the life of the country people which she saw changing is discussed in her book "Old West Surrey".

In 1861 Jekyll enrolled as a student at the Kensington School of Art, where she studied for two years. She met, and was influenced by, some of the most important people in the art world, including Ruskin, Watts, Leighton and William de Morgan. She travelled abroad with friends and relations, becoming proficient in many facets of art, a talented painter with a special interest in colour theory.

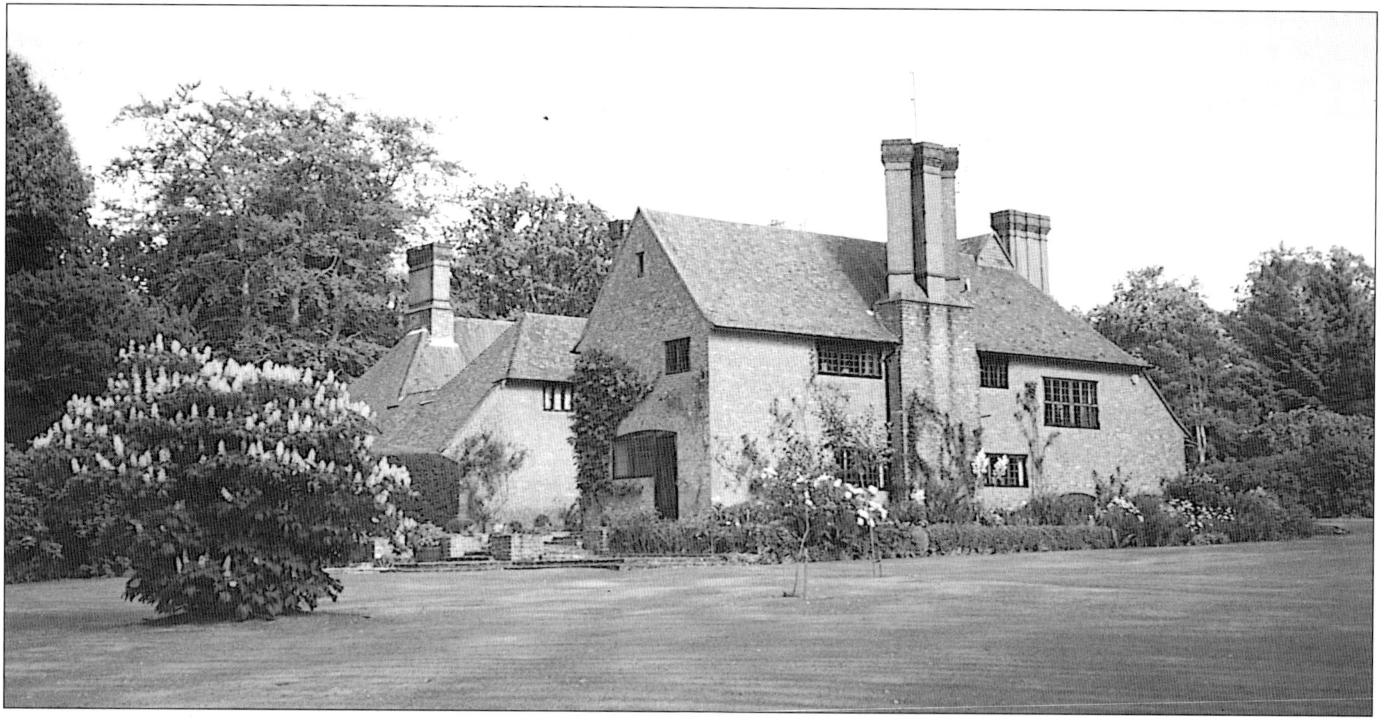

Fig. 40 Jekyll's own house and garden at Munstead Wood. Photographed in 1991

Jekyll's skills also encompassed embroidery and after her work was exhibited at the rooms of the London International Exhibition Society in New Bond Street she received a number of commissions to design curtains and wall hangings.

In 1868 the Jekyll family moved to Wargrave in Berkshire. Here she found the change from her beloved South-West Surrey countryside an unpleasant experience, though the travelling time to London was little changed. In 1869 she went to see William Morris and ever afterwards a well-equipped workshop was a necessity so that she could carry out a range of crafts.

The artist George Leslie who knew her at Wargrave has left an interesting list of her many talents:

> *"...clever and witty in conversation, active and energetic in mind and body and would at all times have shone conspicuously bright among other ladies...there is hardly any useful handicraft the mysteries of which she has not mastered – carving, modelling, house painting, carpentry, smith's work, repousse work, gilding, wood inlaying, embroidery, gardening and all manner of herb and culture...Her artistic taste is very great."* (5)

Jekyll's poor eyesight had been a problem all her life, and it is probable that as close work was becoming a strain, her artistic and design capabilities moved out to the sphere of gardens. Mr Jekyll died in 1876, and her mother moved back to Surrey, having a house built at Munstead Heath, outside Godalming – just a couple of miles from their former home at Bramley.

In 1880 she designed the garden at Munstead House for her mother and also a garden at Robertsbridge, for her friend Madame Bodichon. This was the beginning of the career for which she is most famous today – that of garden designer. About this time she also met William Robinson, the champion of the wild as opposed to the formal garden, who was editor of "The Garden" for which she began to contribute articles. Country Life magazine appeared in 1897 and Jekyll wrote pieces for it.

It is said that her mother began to tire of Jekyll's constant stream of visitors, and in 1884 Jekyll bought 15 acres of heathland across the road from Munstead House, where she first laid out a garden and later had her own home built.

In 1885 Jekyll took up photography and, as with everything she did, soon became proficient, her photographs appearing in "The Garden" magazine, 'Country Life' and in later editions of "The English Flower Garden" by William Robinson.

> *"Refusal to be satisfied until a process was mastered was basic to the Arts and Crafts. In October one of Gertrude's photographs was acknowledged among four joint winners of a competition run by "The Garden". It showed cedar-planted lawns at Peper Harow, the Middletons' park which she had loved since childhood."* (6)

The design of her own garden, at what was to become Munstead Wood, was well advanced when in 1889 she drove to Littleworth Cross near Seale, to take tea with Harry Mangles, the rhododendron enthusiast, whose great collection of natural and hybrid rhododendrons are still maintained in the garden he established there. The young man she met there was Edwin Lutyens and the meeting had a profound effect on both their lives. Lutyens described his first meeting with Miss Jekyll many years after they took tea together in Harry Mangles' garden, commenting that Miss Jekyll had a stern appearance and was dressed "in her Go-To-Meeting Frock – a bunch of cloaked propriety topped by a black felt hat...from which sprang alert black, cock's tail feathers, curving and ever prancing forwards." (7) Apparently, Miss Jekyll did not utter a word to the young architect during the entire afternoon and only as she stepped into her pony cart did she invite him to tea the following week. Thus began the legendary partnership between the twenty year old architect and the fifty year old lady gardener which was to last until Miss Jekyll's death in 1932.

Miss Jekyll and Ned Lutyens had similar philosophies of design and a shared love of the landscape and old buildings of South-West Surrey. They spent many afternoons exploring local villages and beauty spots. It was clear to Miss Jekyll that

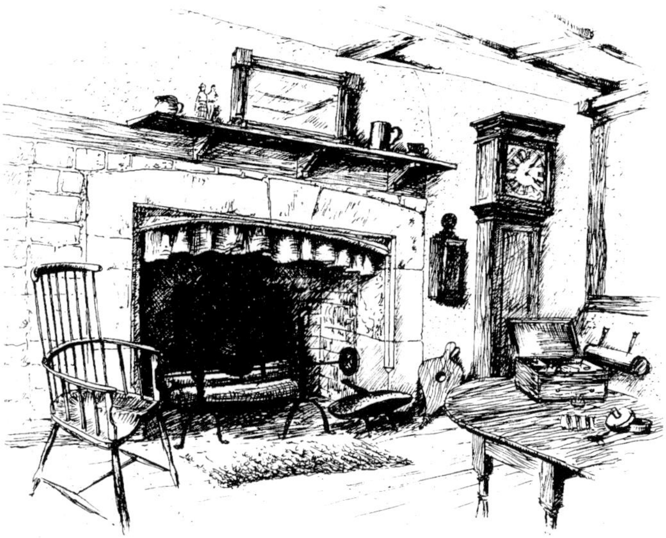

Fig. 41 Sketch of a west Surrey cottage interior containing items collected by Gertrude Jekyll in the Guildford Museum.

her idyllic corner of Surrey was rapidly losing its rural character and she photographed the modest cottages and shops, wild flowers, kitchen gardens and practical implements of country life. Many of the photographs were reproduced in her book 'Old West Surrey' and a selection from her collection of practical implements and furniture, which she gave to the Surrey Archaeological Society, can be seen in the Guildford Museum.

Lutyens designed for her the home she always wanted and she, with her knowledge of plants and designers eye for scale and contrast in foliage and appreciation of colour, could add the finishing touches to his formal garden designs. Together they created, in Jane Brown's words, "Gardens of a Golden Afternoon". Her own garden at Munstead Wood, which she worked at for forty years, became famous in her lifetime, because of her books, such as 'Wood and Garden: Notes and Thoughts, Practical and Critical, of a Working Amateur', 1899; 'Home and Garden', 1900; 'Wall and Water Gardens', 1901; and 'Colour in the Flower Garden', 1908, and articles which appeared in 'The Garden' (1881-1927), 'Gardening Illustrated' (1881-1932) and 'Country Life' magazine (1901-1928), as well as being recorded in her own photographs, and paintings by Helen Allingham and George Elgood.

The garden contained a number of features to be found in Arts and Crafts gardens: Bargate stone wall, pergola, tank, and yew hedges. The only surviving ornament is a lion mask waterspout designed by George Leslie, but terracotta remains have recently been discovered, from which the Martineau bird bath from the Compton pottery and a number of garden pots can be identified, similar to those adjoining the Tank garden which were photographed by Jekyll. (8)

There had also been a topiary cat (cats were her favourite animals).

> *"Gertrude was slightly apologetic about the yew cat, since her garden, she owned, was unsuited for topiary. Nor had it been intended. But some yews at the end of a clump of shrubs grew into a form that suggested some kind of bold sculptural treatment and naturally enough a cat developed."* (9)

Gertrude Jekyll died in 1932, and her life and work are commemorated in both Guildford and Godalming Museums.(10)

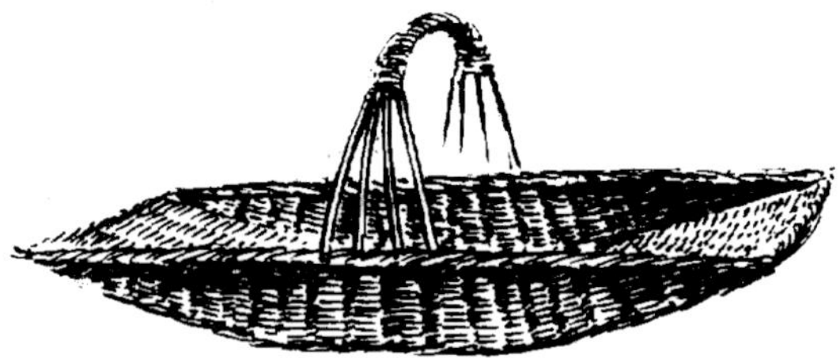

Fig. 42 Munstead Basket: Gertrude Jekyll designed this flower basket and had it made locally by F Cobbet 92A High Street Guildford. It was available in several sizes and advertised for sale in "The Garden Magazine" in 1901, the year that Jekyll was editor of the magazine.

GUILDFORD GARDENS DESIGNED BY GERTRUDE JEKYLL

HIGHMOUNT

In 1909 Jekyll undertook to design the garden at Highmount for the owner Mr Walter Neall. The architect for the house was D. G. Round and the steeply sloping site had impressive views to the south of Guildford. The views are still beautiful today, but the construction of new houses has subdivided the garden and even the original house has been divided into two flats.

Here Jekyll recommended digging into the chalk hillside to create reasonable terraced areas and steep retaining walls. Despite the loss of the bowling green, the croquet lawn and the Spring Garden and the problems involved in subdividing the garden between the houses, a surprising amount of this impressive garden survives. The pergolas still remain, together with the garden house and many of the stone walls, steps, walks and pools. The dry stone walls contain the descendants of Jekyll's original white campanulas, and badgers still play havoc with the lawns.

In Richard Bisgrove's book, "The Gardens of Gertrude Jekyll", (11) he mentioned that almost thirty plans were supplied for Highmount, including one for the roof of the garden shed. Based on her experience of growing plants on a shed roof at Munstead Wood, Jekyll produced a design composed of a number of varieties of "sedum" in her usual planting drifts. Highmount is also mentioned in Miss Jekyll's notebooks which are held at Godalming Museum. She returned to sites she had designed and at Highmount, probably in 1911, at the age of 68 she assessed the planting scheme thus:

"Wall at back wants blue – edge next steps empty – more polygonum comp. a little way back more Camp. carp above landing & opposite – more Allysum... Thereafter more Yuccas – west edge especially wants more to fill among Box bushes." (12)

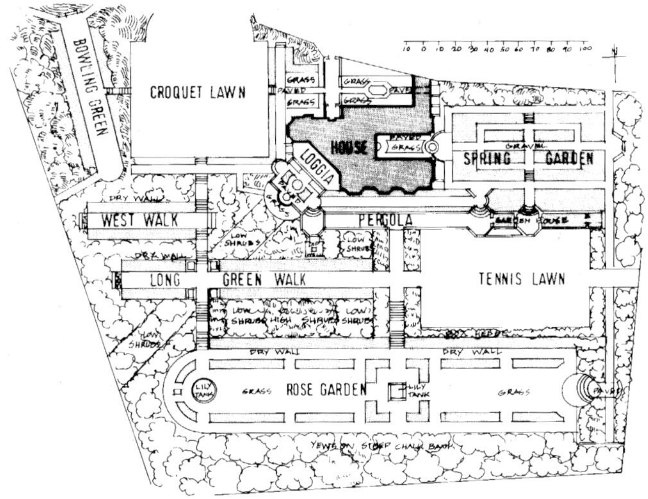

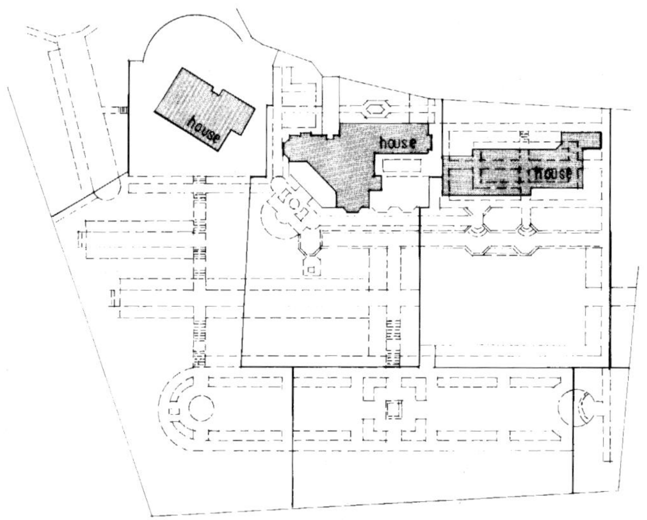

Figs. 43a, 43b Two plans of Highmount grounds, one showing the original Jekyll layout of 1909 and the other showing the subsequent subdivision of the garden, and new buildings.

HILLTOP

According to the present owner, the house was built in 1905 by Higlett, the local builder. Mrs. Walter Neall, who lived at Highmount, further down the road, moved to Hilltop when she was widowed, and asked Miss Jekyll to design the garden for her in 1921.
The garden is featured in Fenja Gunn's book "Lost Gardens of Gertrude Jekyll".

> *"Hilltop is an attractive Edwardian family house... with a garden arranged on different levels overlooking the Surrey landscape. The views are spectacular, particularly as, even today, there are few buildings to be seen... The garden is only an acre in size but is cleverly designed to make the most of its site. It still retains the layout designed for it by Jekyll but, although the garden is richly and variously planted so that it remains full of charm and interest, the original planting has mostly disappeared. Nevertheless, as I went round the garden with the owner, we spotted clumps of Acanthus spinosus in exactly the position planned for it by Jekyll."*(13)

BRADSTONE BROOK

This large mansion in extensive grounds near Shalford Common dates from 1791, but has been added to over the years. In 1921, Miss Jekyll was asked to redesign the gardens for the owner, Mrs. C. M. Wigan, and her drawings survive, along with many of Jekyll's plans, in the Reef Point Gardens Collection. (14) A surveyor's plan of the formal garden to the south of the house shows a bowling green, a pergola, a flower bed containing a dovecote, a number of grass walks and flower beds, and existing oaks and a thorn.

Miss Jekyll's plans show the retention of the pergola, crossed by double herbaceous borders enclosed by hedges. The bowling green and flower beds to the north of it are rationalized into simplified beds (possibly for roses) and enclosed by semi-circular hedging.

The 1934 O.S. 1:25 inch scale indicates a sundial and the southern enclosing hedgeline.

Very little of Miss Jekyll's designs for Bradstone Brook survive, as the requirements of simplified maintenance have made the grassing over of many of her flower beds a necessity. However, the stream side garden which may well predate her contains some beautiful waterside planting. The site contains several excellent specimen trees, and the present gardener has replanted an attractive herbaceous border.

The garden is sometimes open during the summer for charity, and is worthy of a visit.

DURBINS

The house was designed by Roger Fry, for himself, in Guildford. In 1910 he consulted Jekyll on the layout of the garden. Durbins sits just below the ridge of a hilltop, and had outstanding south-facing views (now obscured by more recent development).

> *"A feature of the property was the garden falling away to the south of the house and 'landscaped'; it was planned down to the smallest details by that artist of gardens and gardening, Miss Jekyll. It was built at four descending terraced levels flanked by two large and long buttressed projections faced with dry walls of rough Bargate stone in the interstices of which were planted aubrietias and allysums and other rock plants, which were a glorious show in spring. Monthly roses and lavender crowned the buttresses and a square pond with water lilies mirrored the house in the third terrace. There was plenty of room for fruit and vegetables and grand herbaceous borders where Fry's favourite oriental poppies, blue anchusa and artichokes grew in profusion. In 1910 Fry commissioned Eric Gill to carve a statue of Cupid for the garden, and this artist also made a figure of two lovers destined for the same site in 1911 and a Madonna and child which was designed for indoors."* (15) *(See Fig. XVI. Colour illustration. Durbins, house designed by Roger Fry for himself in 1910. Gertrude Jekyll was consulted on the garden, some features remain)*

HATCHLANDS

Hatchlands, at West Clandon, was built in 1756 for Admiral Boscowan and his wife Fanny, designed by the architect Stiff Leadbetter, and decorated by the young Robert Adam. About 1800, the park was 'improved' by Humphrey Repton, and the Red Book, showing his proposals for the site, still exists.

The owner in 1900 was Lord Rendel, who asked Miss Jekyll's advice on flower gardens adjacent to the house. The result was a scheme for both the south and west parterres. Detailed notes on the drawing shows how deeply the schemes had been thought through, and give solutions for problems such as changes in level. Referring to the fountain on the western access, Jekyll wrote:

> *"Fountain as now has a dull and gloomy look with its high parapet covered with ivy and would be much better with two broad steps, the outer 2 inches above path level, the inner at water level: from that 15 inches to bottom. The cross path now comes in at an awkward angle. Wherever it goes to it should join the other work at a true right angle."* (16)

The design for the South Garden was carried out, that to the west in a very simplified form, and only as far as the fountain, not beyond it as she proposed. Instead of her elaborate beds, simple rectangular beds were made, and a semi-circular hedge planted around the fountain.

In 1914 she was asked to provide detailed planting plans for the South Garden, for Lord Rendel's grandson, the architect, H.S. Goodhart-Rendel who had inherited Hatchlands.

The first plan, bright and cheerful in red, orange and yellow, containing canna, coreopsis, marigolds and calceolaria was annotated; 'this proposed arrangement too late as they are away in August'. The second plan, which was implemented, was for a June garden, and contains roses, peonies, tree lupins, catmint, columbines and iris. In 1919-20 Goodhart-Rendel changed the design of the west parterre, replacing it with a design consisting of six paths radiating from a central fountain. The style was similar to Reginald Blomfield's (author of "The Formal Garden in England") and it is possible that he may have been involved in the design.

Goodhart-Rendel gave Hatchlands to the National Trust in 1945. In recent years a programme of garden restoration has been undertaken and in 1989 work began on re-creating Miss Jekyll's design for the South Garden.

The plans were available, as was detailed information on the plants from one of her notebooks held in the Godalming Museum, but in the last 75 years certain plants have disappeared from nursery catalogues, and finding a source for those specified has proved very difficult in some cases.

Six hundred box plants have been used to make the dwarf hedging around the beds, but the white tree lupin has proved hard to track down.

The South Garden is now complete and planted as nearly as is possible today to Miss Jekyll's specification. Though Miss Jekyll did designs for a number of gardens now in the care of the National Trust, it is believed that this is the first true restoration scheme to be carried out by them to her original drawings. *(See Fig. XIV Colour illustration. The South Garden at Hatchlands which has recently been restored by the National Trust to Gertrude Jekyll's original design)*

ROYAL HORTICULTURAL SOCIETY'S GARDENS, WISLEY

George Frederick Wilson (1822-1902) was a London businessman and managing director of Price's Patent Candle Company. He was a chemist, but his main love was gardening. In 1878 G. F. Wilson bought the estate called 'Oakwood', and began to lay out his ideal garden. Jekyll advised on planting in his gardens, both at Weybridge and Oakwood.

> *"It was in the natural oak wood (which gave the estate its name) that Wilson made his famous wild garden. Amongst the existing oaks and birches he planted masses of rhododendrons and azaleas, as well as other flowering shrubs, conifers and herbaceous plants. He also established primroses, gentians and numerous bulbs, notably Japanese lilies, which...were one of his great passions...*

To the south and north-east of the wild garden, Wilson constructed pools, and these he filled with water lilies, planting Japanese irises and Gunnera around the margins. Contemporary photographs show these areas, and the rustic bridge on which Japanese Wisteria was trained so that the long racemes could hang into the water, looking remarkably similar to today. This, in fact, is not surprising as the Royal Horticultural Society Council decided that the Wild Garden and its immediate surroundings should, as far as possible, be preserved and continued in a manner which would have pleased Wilson." (17)

The storms of 1987 and 1990 which changed so much of the gardens of Surrey altered parts of Wisley out of all recognition. However, the Royal Horticultural Society gardens are a wonderful resource, containing plant specimens from throughout the world, and examples of all styles of gardening. Expert advice on all aspects of gardening, plant identification and pest control is on hand, as well as a well stocked book and gift shop, and plant centre.

GARDEN INFLUENCES ON ARTS AND CRAFTS ARCHITECTS

GREAT TANGLEY MANOR, NEAR GUILDFORD

One house and garden which would have been well known to Jekyll was Great Tangley Manor. In 1884 Wickham Flower bought the derelict sixteenth century manor house and employed Philip Webb to repair and enlarge the house. The gardens were laid out in 1884, both within the moat which surrounds the house, and beyond it.

The scale and quality of the garden improvements are described in this contemporary account.

"A body of about 18 labouring men worked under directions given to them week by week, and the gardens and grounds were completed within a period of about 6 months. The leading idea was evidently to produce a natural arrangement in proper keeping of character and

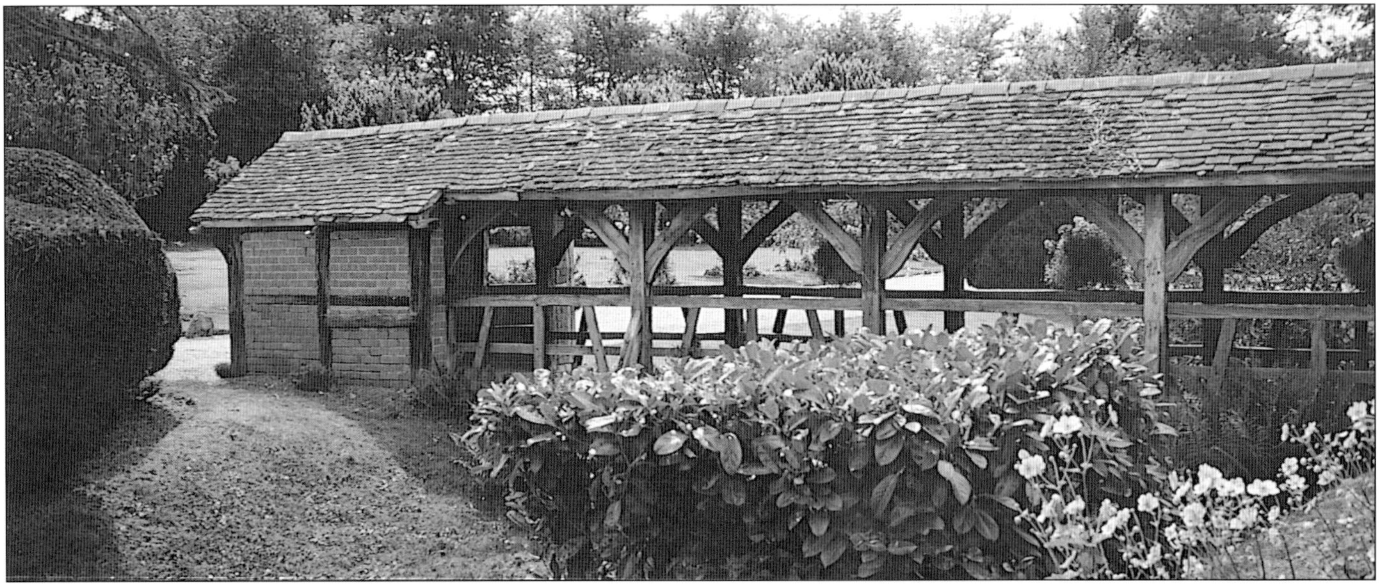

Fig. 44 Covered footbridge across the moat at Great Tangley Manor designed by Philip Webb in 1884

quaintness with the house.

But it is a sin against Nature and against Art alike to attempt the impossible or to persist in trying to grow that which will not thrive, but will at best be poor, stunted and insignificant. The capacities of a place must be considered thoughtfully, else will the result be certain failure.

Take Tangley Manor for all in all, it is certainly one of the most beautiful pleasaunces in England, and a true work of natural art." (18)

Such was the impact of the property that Country Life carried no less than three articles about it and Gertrude Jekyll's and G.S. Elgood's book, "Some English Gardens", of 1905 also mentions it.

Country Life, the premier magazine of the period, gave publicity to the Arts and Crafts Movement and particularly to the work of Lutyens, and associated gardens.

Two books which had a profound influence on architects who designed gardens with their houses were Thomas Mawson's "Art and Craft of Garden Making" (1900) which went through four editions before the First World War and G. Jekyll's and L. Weaver's "Gardens for Small Country Houses" (1912). The introduction to "Gardens for Small Country Houses" (19) sets out a number of the principles of Arts and Crafts gardens, with headings such as "Relation of garden to house, Importance of preserving or creating character, Misuse of conifers, Beauty of native evergreens... yew and other hedges... treillage". The book contains information on all aspects of garden design. There is a chapter on ornaments, statues and vases, sundials and seats; also guidance on garden houses, gates and gateways, pergolas, paving and retaining walls and their planting. It also discusses in detail two important Guildford gardens – Highmount, designed by Jekyll, and Littleholme, the Voysey house built for Mr Muntzer. *(See p. 59, Highmount and p. 64, Littleholme)*

ARTS AND CRAFTS ARCHITECTS AND GARDEN DESIGNERS

NORMAN SHAW

MERRIST WOOD

Merrist Wood Hall, built in 1877 by Norman Shaw, was owned by the Shrubb family, and had its own estate of woodlands and timbered park-like grounds. Many of the fine trees around the buildings date from this period: such as the Wellingtonia, oaks, cedars and copper beeches on the sloping south-west lawns.

PICCARDS ROUGH

Piccards Rough was designed by Norman Shaw in 1887, and like many other imposing houses of this time was situated on a ridge of high ground, with south facing views.

By 1896 the garden had been laid out in a series of enclosures, with formal pathways, yew hedges, a fountain, sundials, walls and steps. The main southern slope was lawn, containing some specimen trees.

Today, the main house has been divided into two units, and the subdivision of the garden, together with a swimming pool and tennis court, make it difficult to imagine the garden to the south of the main house as it was.

Fortunately, the garden to the west of the house is now attached to what was the gardener's cottage. This contains the immaculately trimmed yew hedges and borders which were designed to complement Piccards Rough. In the loving hands of the present owners the garden has grown to maturity, and retains a serene Edwardian atmosphere.

A secret Japanese garden still contains seats produced at the Compton Pottery, as illustrated, outside the workshop early this century. (*See Fig. XVII Colour illustration. Compton Pottery seats in the Japanese Garden at Piccards Rough and Fig. 39b, The Pottery Works p. 55*)

Fig. 45 Greyfriars, Guildford: view along the west garden terrace designed by Herbert Baker.

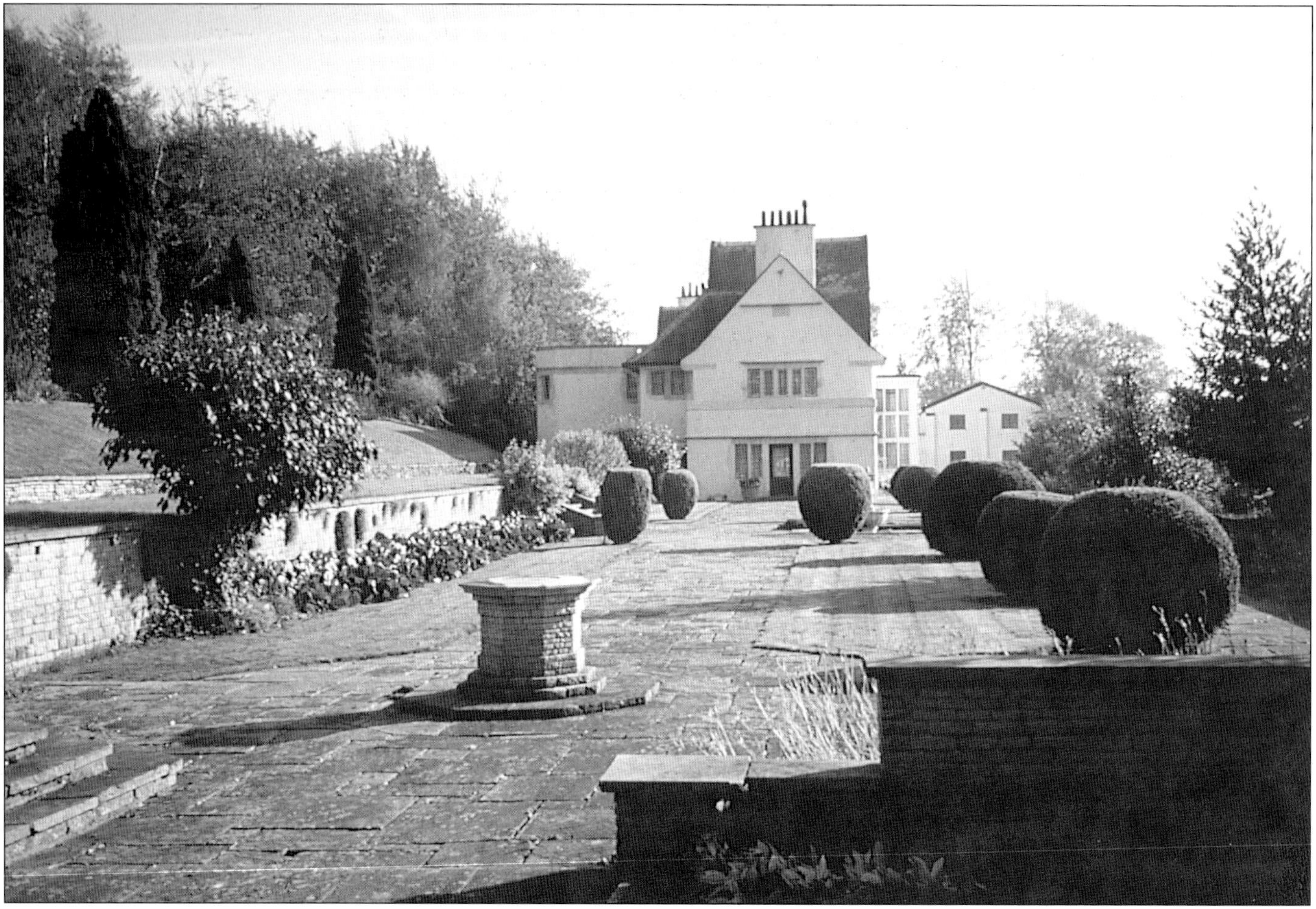

VOYSEY

LITTLEHOLME

At Littleholme in Guildford the gardens were laid out by Thomas Young of Woking in association with Voysey, who was the architect for the house.

Young had a large water storage tank installed under the central stone paved patio to ensure that the chalky soil received enough water. Other garden features are two seats designed by Voysey by the pond and, at the front entrance, two original terracotta pots from the Compton Pottery.

The site is now much reduced from that illustrated in "Gardens for Small Country Houses" – not only has the house been divided into three, but new houses have been built to the east and west and in the fruit gardens at the lower end of the site. Despite the problems of subdivision this remains an excellent Arts and Crafts garden.

The southerly views are still impressive, but contain many more buildings than when the house was first built. The site has been cleverly terraced to improve access to it from the road at a higher level, and to create a wide paved terrace, with a pool, sundial and alcoves formed by yew hedges, below the house.

GREYFRIARS

The Voysey house, Greyfriars, sits just below the ridge of the Hog's Back, with outstanding panoramic views to the south.

> *"The long, low roughcast house ties itself self-effacingly into the landscape, and the pleasure to be got in walking around it is that of a continuous interchange between building and landscape, without any single view that can be analysed in detail....*
>
> *The horticultural details are mentioned because, to say it again, the gardens are as important as the house, or rather the two are indivisible....*
>
> *The western extension and present staircase are later additions of 1913 by Herbert Baker, who also did the garden."* (20)

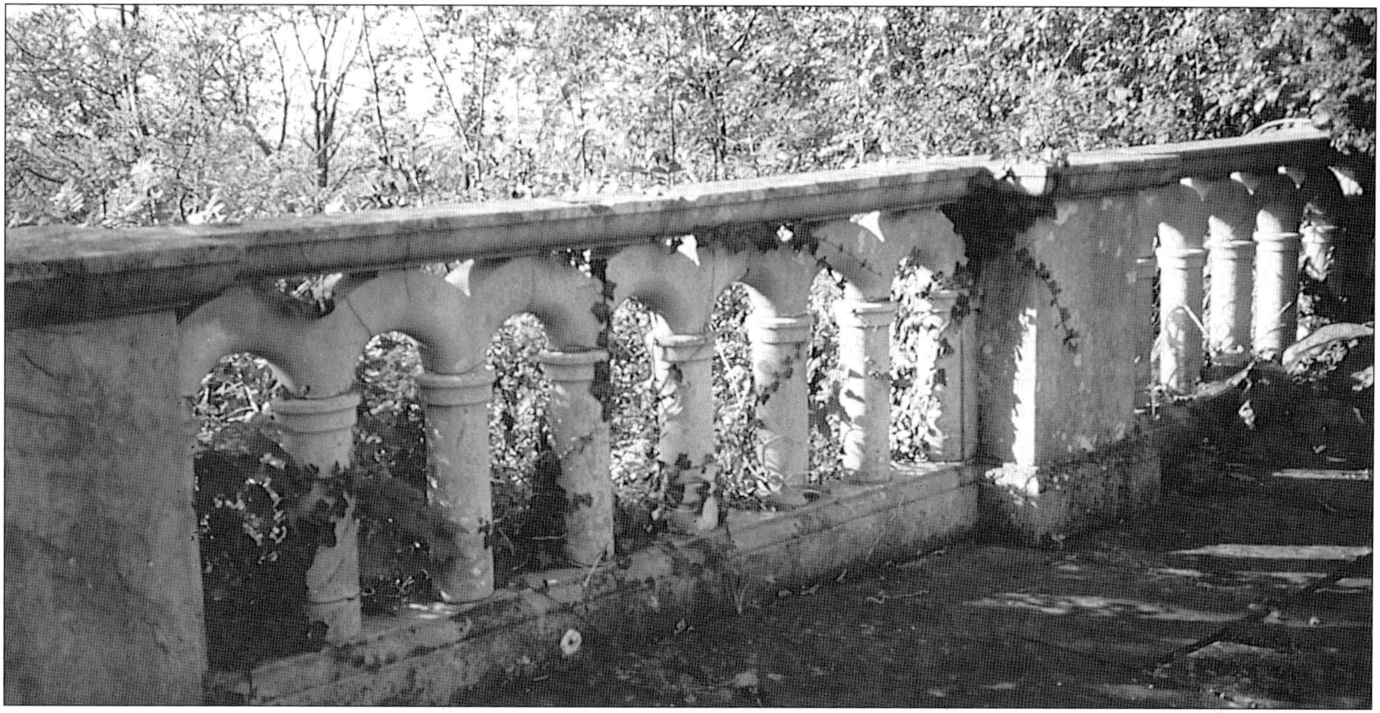

Fig. 46 Greyfriars, Guildford: Balustrade to south terrace.

The garden is essentially linear, making use of the level terraces, which are connected by stone steps. Stone balustrading and hedging give vertical enclosure, and there are considerable areas of stone pathways and steps, as well as pools, summer-houses and topiary balls. It is probable that there were also contemporary pots and vases, but none now survive at the site. The garden also suffered badly in the great storms of 1987 and 1990, the tree loss creating dramatic changes to the privacy of the garden from the main road alongside it.

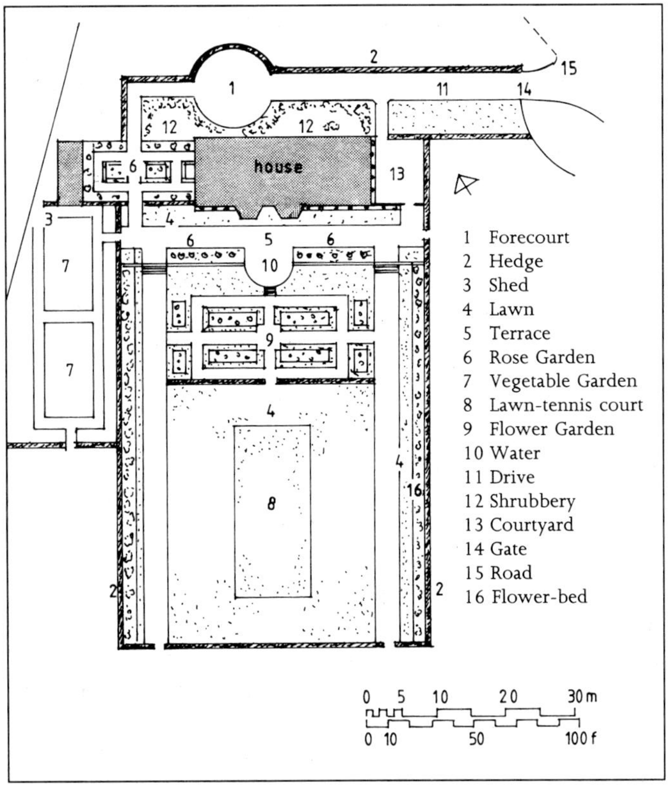

Fig 47 Plan of the garden at Priors Garth (now Priors Field). Planting plans by Gertrude Jekyll (1901) exist in the Reef Point Collection.

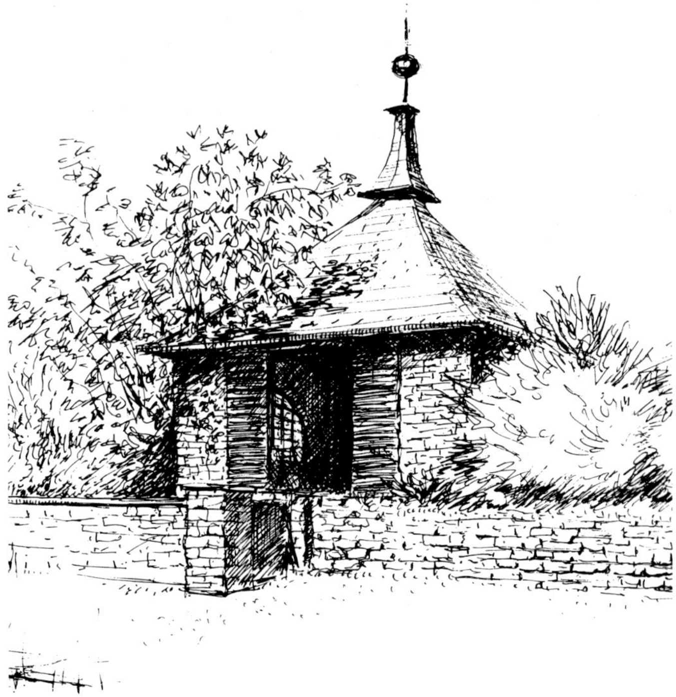

Fig 48 Summerhouse by Voysey (1897) at Norney Grange

NORNEY GRANGE

It is probable that Voysey was involved in the layout of the garden. The sloping site has been terraced below the house with dry stone walling, and stone steps link the levels. Various enclosures have been made with Yew and Beech hedging, and there are two attractive summer-houses in the garden.

THACKERAY TURNER

Jekyll greatly admired the work of the architect Thackeray Turner and a whole chapter in her book "Gardens for Small Country Houses" is devoted to his own garden at Westbrook, Godalming (built 1899). All the features she admired are still there, such as the sunken garden, the pleached lime avenue and the Winter Garden.

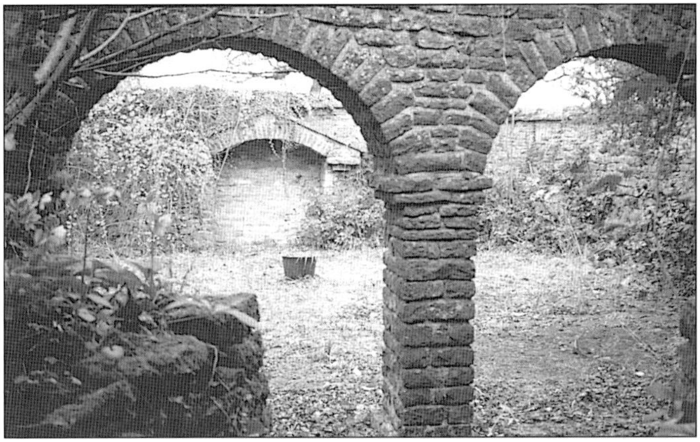

Fig. 49 The Winter Garden at Thackeray Turner's house, Westbrook, today.

Gertrude Jekyll and Thackeray Turner also worked together on the Phillips Memorial, built on the water meadows in Godalming to commemorate the local man who was the radio operator on the Titanic. Thackeray Turner designed the cloister building and Jekyll the planting within the courtyard, now restored to its original plans by Waverley Borough Council and the Surrey Gardens Trust. Thackeray Turner was a talented amateur gardener and in 1913 spoke at the meeting held at the Art Workers Guild, on the History and Making of Gardens. It would have been more appropriate to have had Jekyll as principal speaker, but women were not admitted as members of the Art Workers Guild until 1964. A Jekyll garden also survives in part at Kingswood Hanger near Gomshall, where Thackeray Turner is reputed to have been the architect.

M H BAILLIE SCOTT

Jekyll prepared designs for the garden at Garden Court, Guildford, in 1915, for which plans survive in the Reef Point Collection at Berkeley.

Baillie Scott designed Garden Court and the adjacent house, now subdivided (Quarry Heights and Undershaw). Much of the lower garden has been lost to development.

He was a talented artist, and illustrated in watercolour many of his commissions. *(See Baillie Scott's watercolour of Undershaw on the front cover)*

Baille Scott had decided views on flowers:

> *"The possessor of such a little garden will find scope enough within its boundaries to create a little paradise of flowers. But it should always be borne in mind that the flowers are for the garden, not the garden for the flowers."*

Jekyll was an important influence:

> *"To those who wish to study the subject I would recommend a careful perusal of Miss Jekyll's books which may be taken as an infallible guide."* (21)

PICCARDS MANOR

Piccards Manor was known as Piccards Farm, and was just that: a farmhouse, surrounded by a number of farm buildings and barns, part of the Loseley estate.

In the 1930s the property was bought by three ladies named Howarth, daughters of a wealthy Liverpool merchant. One of them was a very keen gardener, and laid out the gardens as they are today. (22) To the south of the house the barns and perimeter wall give enclosure to the terraced garden, while to the east is the more formal garden containing a pool.

Though strictly speaking designed outside the 'Arts and Crafts' era, the buildings and gardens are in such unity of style and material that it is only right to include them. The clipped hedges of box and yew, the stonework, and the design of the garden around the house and buildings are typical of the Arts and Crafts Movement. *(See Fig. XVIII Colour illustration Piccards Manor: An example of an Arts and Crafts style garden added to complement an existing sixteenth century farmhouse)*

NOTES:

(1) Taken from 'Gardens for Small Country Houses' by Gertrude Jekyll and Lawrence Weaver, Ch XIX, Statues and Vases, p 223.
(2) 'England's Michelangelo, A Biography of George Frederick Watts' by Wilfrid Blunt, 1975
(3) 'Country Life', March 15, 1902.
(4) 'The Potters Arts Guild', Mrs G F Watts' Village Industry, Compton, Guildford
(5) 'Gertrude Jekyll: A Memoir' by Francis Jekyll.
(6) 'Gertrude Jekyll', Sally Festing, Viking 1991, p 104.
(7) 'Gardens of a Golden Afternoon. The Story of a Partnership: Edwin Lutyens & Gertrude Jekyll', Jane Brown, 1982.
(8) 'Gertrude Jekyll. A Vision of Garden and Wood' by Judith B Tankard and Michael R Van Valkenburgh (page 77, photograph published 1908).
(9) 'Gertrude Jekyll', Sally Festing, Viking, 1991.
(10) Gertrude Jekyll gave her collection of household items to the Surrey Archaeological Society, and a selection is on display in Guildford Museum.
(11) 'The Gardens of Gertrude Jekyll' by Richard Bisgrove.
(12) 'Gertrude Jekyll's Garden Note Books', Sally Festing, 'Hortus' Spring 1991.
(13) 'Lost Gardens of Gertrude Jekyll' by Fenja Gunn.
(14) Reef Point Gardens Collection, at the Documents Collection, College of Environmental Design, University of California, Berkeley, 94720, U.S.A.
A microfilm of the collection can be consulted at the R.C.H.M., Fortress House, Savile Row, London. A photocopied set is housed at Godalming Museum, Surrey.
(15) 'Letters of Roger Fry', (ed) Denys Sutton, Vol (ii), Chatto, 1972.
(16) 'Gertrude Jekyll' by Sally Festing. Pages 154-155.
(17) 'Wisley, the Royal Horticultural Society's Garden' by Martyn and Alison Rix, 1989.
(18) 'Gardens Old and New, the Country House and Its Garden Environment.'
(19) 'Gardens for Small Country Houses', Gertrude Jekyll and Lawrence Weaver (1912). Contents page.
(20) 'The Buildings of England: Survey by Ian Nairn & Nikolaus Pevsner', revised by Bridget Cherry.
(21) 'The Edwardian Garden', David Ottewill, 1989. P 137.
22) 'In an Elizabethan Country Garden...', article by Sally Festing in The Advertiser, May 2, 1974.

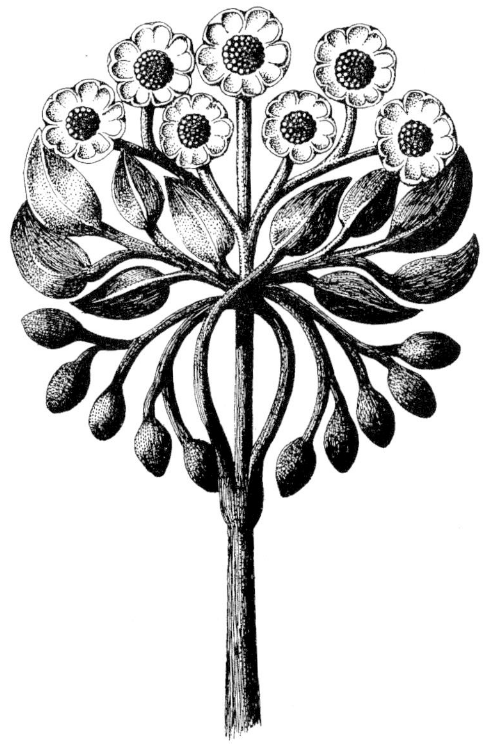

Fig 50: Sketch of Firedog designed by Baillie Scott

ARTS AND CRAFTS BUILDINGS, GARDENS AND MUSEUMS OPEN TO THE PUBLIC IN GUILDFORD

As arrangements for visitors may be subject to change,
it is recommended that you check details with the venue before making a visit.

THE *WATTS* GALLERY

Down Lane, Compton, Guildford, GU3 1DQ. Tel: 01483 810235
www.wattsgallery.org.uk Admission Free.

Designed by Christopher Turnor in 1904, the gallery houses a large collection of paintings by Victorian painter G.F. Watts including large allegorical works, some fine portraits of leading Victorian personalities, sculptures and examples of works from the Compton Pottery.

WATTS MEMORIAL CHAPEL

Down Lane, Compton, Guildford, GU3 1DQ.

Designed by Mary Watts in 1896 and donated to the village by Mr and Mrs G.F. Watts. The decorative external terracotta tiles and all internal decoration are to Mrs Watt's designs and executed by local villagers trained by her. There are also several terracotta tombstones and the Watts Memorial Cloister (1911) also designed by Mary Watts.

THE GUILDFORD MUSEUM

Castle Arch, Quarry Street, Guildford; Tel: 01483 444750
www.surreyweb.org.uk/guildfordmuseum. Admission Free.

The museum houses Gertrude Jekyll's personal collection of practical implements and furniture from rural West Surrey which she donated to the Surrey Archeological Society. Miss Jekyll was intensely interested in recording and preserving the traditional tools and aspects of rural lifestyle which was rapidly disappearing. Discover Lewis Caroll's links with the town.

THE THREE PIGEONS PUBLIC HOUSE

High Street, Guildford

The front elevation was designed by T.R. Clements in the Arts and Crafts style for Friary Brewery (circa 1918).
(See Fig. 51)

GERTRUDE JEKYLL GARDEN AT HATCHLANDS PARK (NT)

East Clandon, Guildford GU4 7RT. Tel: 01483 222482.

Hatchlands, (c.1757) with interiors by Robert Adam. Park designed by Humphrey Repton (1800), with early Summer flowering garden restored to Gertrude Jekyll's plans of 1914.

THE LUCKY DUCK TEA ROOM

Middle Street, Shere. Tel: 01483 202445.

Designed (1892) by Sir Edwin Lutyens, the stores have been in continual use for over one hundred years.

MERRIST *WOOD* HOUSE

Merrist Wood Agricultural College, Worplesdon, Surrey.Tel: 01483 884000.

Designed (1876-77) by R. Norman Shaw, originally a country house, can be seen during open day (usually in May).

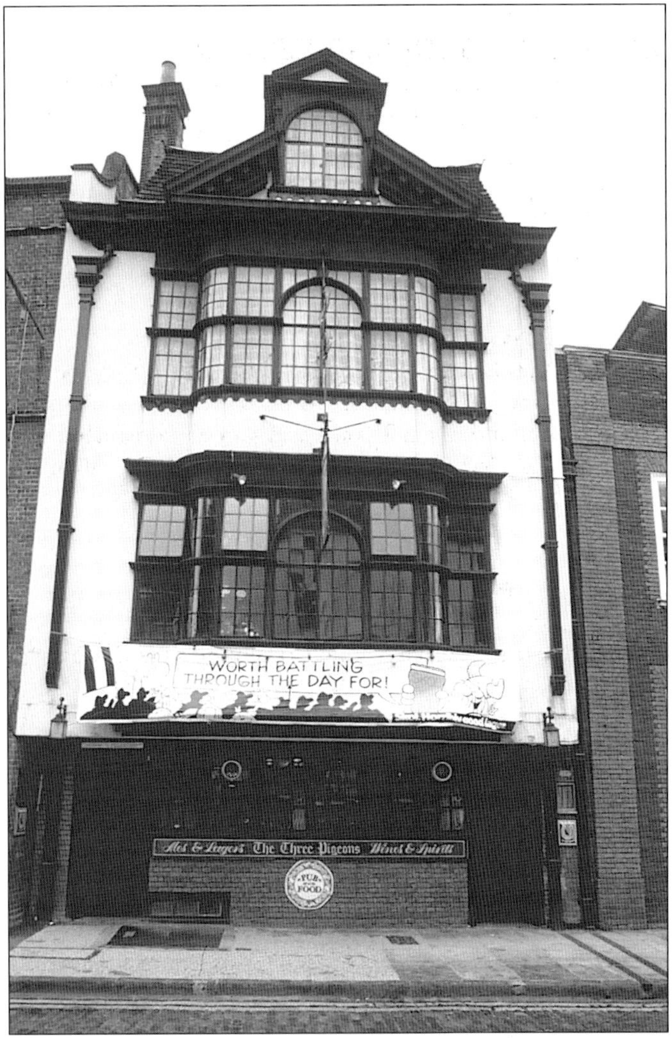

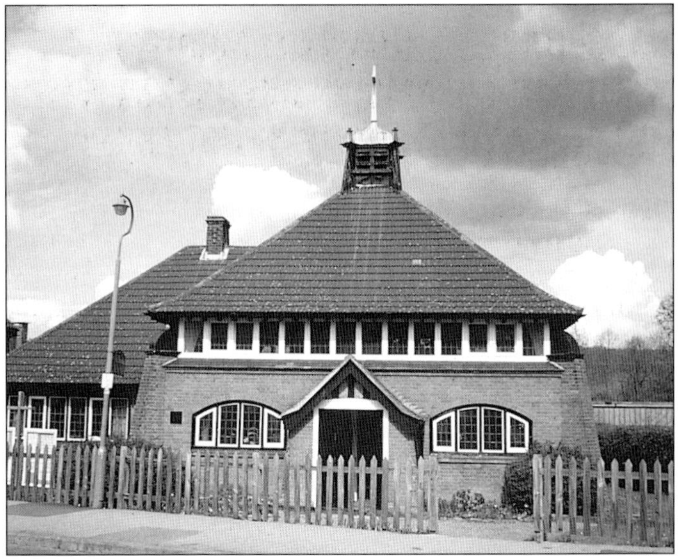

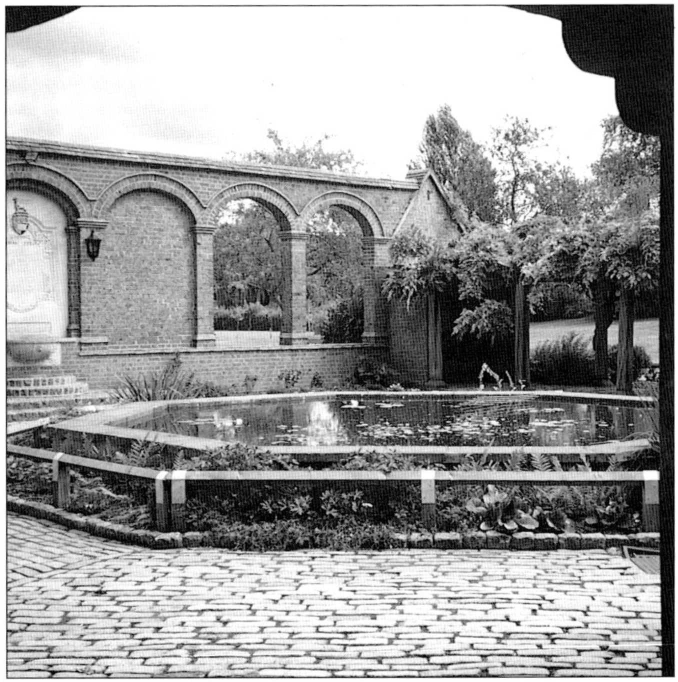

Above: Fig. 51 The Three Pigeons Public House, High Street, Guildford

Top Right: Fig. 52 Church of St Thomas, Chilworth

Right: Fig. 53: The Phillips Memorial 1912, Godalming
(Courtesy of Michael Edwards)

CHURCHES IN GUILDFORD BOROUGH WITH SOME FEATURES REPRESENTATIVE OF THE ARTS AND CRAFTS MOVEMENT

CHURCH OF ST THOMAS

New Road, Chilworth

Designed by W. Seth-Smith, the building originally functioned as an educational Institute and later as a working men's club for the Gunpowder Works in Chilworth. Turned into an Anglican church in 1896, this unique structure with its dramatic pyramidal roof originally had exposed red brick walls internally. A fine example of a communal village building in the Arts and Crafts Style. (See fig. 52)

OCKHAM CHURCH

Contains a memorial to Ralph, second Earl of Lovelace (1906) which is attributed to C.F.A. Voysey; The East Window is by Sir T.G. Jackson (1895).

CHURCH OF ST JAMES, SHERE

The Lychgate at the Church of St James, Shere was designed by Lutyens in 1902; an 1895 vestry addition is attributed to S. Weatherley.

CHURCH OF ST THOMAS, EAST CLANDON

The church has a bell tower addition and north aisle by Sir T.G. Jackson dating from 1900; H. Goodhart-Rendel designed a Gothic style chest tomb for Baron Rendel of Hatchlands (1913).

CHURCH OF ST PETER AND ST PAUL, WEST CLANDON

The church was restored and a tower added in 1879 by J.C. Boys; the spire was rebuilt in 1913 by Sir T.G. Jackson.

CHURCH OF ST JOHN, GUILDFORD

The church in Stoke Road, Guildford has a window in the North Chapel designed by Dante Gabriel Rossetti in 1888.

VENTURING OUTSIDE GUILDFORD BOROUGH

GODALMING MUSEUM,

109a High Street, Godalming, Surrey GU7 1AQ. Tel: 01483 426510. Admission Free.

The museum has a room devoted to the Jekyll/Lutyens collaboration and a small courtyard garden constucted to a Jekyll design. Copies of Gertrude Jekyll's plans held in the Reef Point Collection are available for reference.

THE PHILLIPS MEMORIAL GARDEN

Borough Road, Godalming

In a gentle setting tucked behind Godalming's Parish Church and the River Wey stands a memorial cloister (c.1912) dedicated to 'Jack' Phillips of Farncombe, the wireless operator aboard the Titanic who stayed at his post and went down with the ship. Designed by architect Thackeray Turner with garden plans by Gertrude Jekyll, the garden has been restored by the Surrey Gardens Trust and Waverley Borough Council. The public can visit at any time. (See Fig. 53)

OAKHURST COTTAGE (NT)

Hambledon, near Godalming. Strictly by appointment; Tel: 01428 683207. Admission with guided tour.

Preserved 19th century labourer's cottage (originally a late 16th century barn). This tiny building is furnished with items from the Gertrude Jekyll Collection and was the subject of a painting by Victorian watercolourist, Helen Allingham.

GODDARDS

Abinger Common, Dorking, Surrey, RH5 6TH. The gardens and library are open by appointment only through The Lutyens Trust. Tel: 01306 730487. Holiday letting information can be obtained from the Landmark Trust, Shottesbrooke, Maidenhead, Berkshire SL6 3SW.

Goddards was designed by Sir Edwin Lutyens for Frederick Mirrielees who commissioned the building as a rest home for "ladies of small means". Completed in 1900, Goddards became a family home with later additions by Lutyens in 1910. The house with its beautifully kept gardens designed by Gertrude Jekyll is an idyllic example of Arts and Crafts principles and of the collaboration of Lutyens and Jekyll. (See Fig 54)

ROYAL HORTICULTURAL SOCIETY'S WISLEY GARDENS

Off the A3 north of Guildford; Gardens are open all week to RHS members. Tel: 01483 224234

The main buildings date from 1914 by architects Imrie & Angell in a Tudor style derivative from Lutyens. The original 60 acre site was purchased in the late nineteenth century by G.F. Wilson who planned it as a natural garden in consultation with Gertrude Jekyll. The garden was bequeathed to the Royal Horticultural Society in 1903.

STANDEN, WEST SUSSEX (NT)

Located on the B2110, 2 miles south of East Grinstead in West Sussex. Tel: 01342 323029.

A country house designed by Philip Webb in 1892. A fine example of Arts and Crafts architecture which contains many original wallpapers, fabrics and carpets by William Morris. Collections of original and added Arts and Crafts furnishings and craftworks are on display including William de Morgan pottery, furniture by Ernest Gimson and the original electric light fittings from 1892.

BRIGHTON MUSEUM AND ART GALLERY

Located in the grounds of the Brighton Pavilion, Church Street, Brighton BN1 1UE. Tel: 01273 603005. www.brighton-hove.gov.uk/bhc/museums/brighton

The Art Nouveau and Art Deco gallery contains furniture and artifacts from Littleholme, the Guildford house designed by C.F.A. Voysey (1907). Other Arts and Crafts objects on display are by Charles Rennie Mackintosh and from the Liberty collection.

WILLIAM MORRIS GALLERY

Water House, Lloyd Park, Forest Road, Walthamstow, London E17 4PP. Tel: 020 8527 3782. www.lbwf.gov.uk/wmg

18th century Water House was William Morris's family home between 1848 and 1856. Now a museum housing a major collection illustrating the achievements and influences of Morris and the Arts and Crafts Movement. There are permanent displays of printed and woven fabrics, rugs, carpets, wallpapers, furniture, stained glass and tiles designed by Morris himself, and others who founded the firm of Morris, Marshall, Faulkner and Company in 1861.

VICTORIA AND ALBERT MUSEUM,

Cromwell Road, South Kensington, London SW7 2RL. Tel: 020 7835 1715. www.vam.ac.uk.

Major collections of artifacts, textiles, wallpaper and furniture representative of the Arts and Crafts Movement are permanently exhibited including the 'Green Dining Room', designed by William Morris, which served as one of the V&A's original refreshment rooms.

GEFFRYE MUSEUM,

Kingsland Road, London E2 8AE. Tel: 020 7739 9893. www.geffrye-museum.org.uk Free admission.

Housed in almhouses built in 1715, the museum is devoted to displays of domestic interiors from 1600 to 1990 including an Edwardian room.

MUNSTEAD WOOD, GODALMING

Consult the National Gardens Scheme 'Yellow Book', an annual publication, for further details. Tel: 01493 211535. www.ngs.org.uk

10 acres of rhododendrons, azaleas, shrubs and flower borders planned by Gertrude Jekyll. The house (not open) was designed by Sir Edward Lutyens and was Miss Jekyll's home.

VANN, HAMBLEDON

Consult the National Gardens Scheme 'Yellow Book', an annual publication, for further details. Tel: 01493 211535. www.ngs.org.uk

English Heritage registered garden of 4 ½ acres surrounding a Tudor/William and Mary house (not open) with later additions by WD Caroe. The garden includes a Gertrude Jekyll water garden of 1911.

HEATHERSETT, LITTLEWORTH CROSS

Consult the National Gardens Scheme 'Yellow Book', an annual publication, for further details. Tel: 01493 211535. www.ngs.org.uk

Historic 25 acre woodland garden created at the end of the 19th century by HJ Mangles, an early hybridiser of rhododendrons. Where Lutyens first met Gertrude Jekyll. Fowl house designed by Edwin Lutyens in the garden. See Figs.V &VI Colour illustrations.

KELMSCOTT HOUSE

26 Upper Mall, Hammersmith, London W6 9TA. Tel: 020 8741 3735. www.morrissociety.org

Home of William Morris from 1878 - 1896 and now the headquarters of the William Morris Society, which has its office and libary in the coach house, (limited opening to the public). Membership offers lectures and visits, a quarterly newsletter, bi-annual journal and use of the extensive library

THE MUSEUM OF DOMESTIC DESIGN & ARCHITECTURE

Middlesex University, Cat Hill, Barnet, Hertfordshire. Tel: 020 8411 5244. www.moda.mdx.ac.uk

MODA holds an outstanding collection of wallpapers, textiles, photographs and furnishing catalogues offering a vivid picture of late nineteenth and twentieth century design for the home. MODA holds six collections of which the largest is the Silver Studio Collection, an archive of a commercial design practice that operated in London from 1891 to 1963. There is a permanent exhibition, 'Exploring Interiors: Decoration of the Home 1900 - 1960' and a regular programme of changing exhibitions and events.

KELMSCOTT MANOR

Kelmscott, Nr Lechlade, Oxfordshire, GL7 3HJ. Tel: 01367 252486. www.kelmscottmanor.co.uk

Now owned by the Society of Antiquaries of London. Kelmscott Manor, a 16/17th century stone farmhouse was the country home of William Morris - poet, craftsman and socialist - from 1871 until his death in 1896. The house, eulogised in Morris's novel *News from Nowhere*, contains a collection of the possessions and works of Morris and his associates, including furniture, textiles, carpets and ceramics. Also in the village are the Memorial Cottages (1902) designed by architect Philip Webb, the Morris Memorial Hall designed by architect Ernest Gimson and Morris's tomb, also by Webb, in St George's Churchyard.

RODMARTON MANOR

Rodmarton, near Cirencester, GL55 6PF. Tel: 01285 841253. www.rodmarton-manor.co.uk

One of the finest achievements of the Arts and Crafts Movement, a house and garden designed by Earnest Barnsley and built between 1909 - 26 for the Hon. Claud Biddulph, with architectural detailing, furniture and furnishings by many of the Cotswolds' most renowed craftsmen.

CHELTENHAM ART GALLERY AND MUSEUM

Clarence Street, Cheltenham, GL50 3JT. Tel: 01242 237431.
www.artsandcraftsmuseum.org.uk

An internationally important collection relating to the British Arts & Crafts Movement with fine furniture, exquisite metalwork and decorative arts from the period and with many examples of the achievements of the Cotswold craftsmen.

BLACKWELL

Bowness-on-Windermere, Cumbria, LA23 3JR. Tel: 015394 46139.
www.blackwell.org.uk

Blackwell is one of the largest and most important surviving Arts and Crafts Movement houses in Britain. Built by the architect MH Baillie Scott for Sir Edward Holt in 1898 - 9 in one of the Lake District's most beautiful settings with views of Lake Windermere and the Coniston fells. The house is a work of art with carved panelling, stained glass and intricate wrought ironwork - all inspired by Lakeland flowers, trees and birds. Blackwell has been saved and restored by the Lakeland Arts Trust and is opened to the public as a gallery with exhibitions of contemporary and historical applied arts and crafts.

BIRMINGHAM MUSEUM AND ART GALLERY

Chamberlain Square, Birmingham B3 3DH. Tel: 0121 303 2834.
www.birmingham.gov.uk/bmag

Outstanding Pre-Raphaelite paintings and drawings, including many of the most famous works and applied arts of the Birmingham Arts and Crafts Movement.

WIGHTWICK MANOR (NT)

Wightwick Bank, Wolverhampton, West Midlands, WV6 8EE. Tel: 01902 761108.

Built 1887 - 93 and one of only a few surviving examples of a house built and furnished under the influence of the Arts and Crafts Movement. The many original William Morris wallpapers and fabrics, Pre-Raphaelite paintings, Kempe glass and de Morgan ware help conjure up the spirit of the time. An attractive garden reflects the style and character of the house.

THE HILL HOUSE (NT)

Upper Colquhoun Street, Helensburgh, Strathclyde G84 9AJ. Tel: 01436 67300.
www.nts.org.uk/hillhouse.html

The finest of Charles Rennie Mackintosh's houses, commissioned by Glasgow publisher Walter Blackie in 1902. Mackintosh also designed the garden, furniture, interior fittings and decorative schemes.

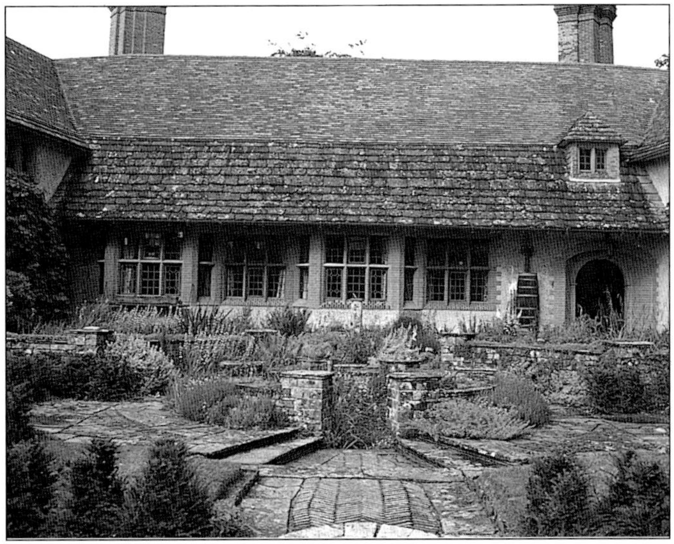

Fig 54 Goddards, Abinger Hammer. Now the headquarters of the Lutyens Trust, the house and garden represent an idyllic example of Arts and Crafts principles and the collaboration of Lutyens and Jekyll.